WORLDWISE 4

Contents

1	The Irish landscape	2
2	Where in the world?	8
3	Have you got the time please?	11
4	Getting the balance right	14
5	Journey into space	22
6	Up with people	29
7	On the streets where you live	34
8	Weatherwatch	39
9	Wonders of the natural world	44
10	Rural life	48
11	Let's play Dublin	51
12	Climate and climatic change	57
13	Water and life	60
14	The explosive earth	65
15	Maps and skills	70
16	Children of the world	74
17	Effortless power – with the flick of a switch	78
18	Little and large ... countries of the world	85
19	Down to earth	89
20	A continent develops	93
21	Changing patterns of industry	98
22	Land of the rising sun – Japan	103
23	Going to the Americas	108
24	Passage to India	116
25	Life down under	122
26	I'd like to see under the sea	127
27	And on to Asia	133
28	Understanding boundaries	138
29	The world family	142

Approved Quality System

The Educational Company

1 The Irish landscape

Hello again. Hasn't time flown? It seems such a short time ago that we first looked at our world in *Worldwise 1*. And yet, here you are, in sixth class and about to embark on your final journey of exploration before going on to second-level school.

If we put your four years of *Worldwise* Geography into the full span of life you can expect to live, they seem very short indeed.
We get the same sort of feeling if we consider our lives against the many, many millions of years it has taken the landscape of our countryside to develop.

THE BURREN

One of the most interesting parts of the Irish landscape is the region in the north of Co. Clare known as the Burren. Place-names can tell us much about a landscape. The name Burren comes from an Irish word – *Boireann*. This means a rocky place and at first look that is just how it seems.

But on looking closer we discover that the Burren landscape is a treasure-chest of surprises. What seems to be a bleak moon-like landscape is extremely rich in plant and animal life. Of the 1,400 different plants that grow in Ireland 1,100 are found in the Burren. Only two out of the thirty kinds of Irish butterfly are not found there.

LIMESTONE ROCK

Limestone is the most common rock in Ireland. In most parts of the country it is covered with soil or earth. In the Burren we can see large blocks of the limestone exposed and uncovered. Limestone was formed from the shells of sea-animals who lived in the shallow seas about 300 million years ago. At that time the position of Ireland was not the same as it is now. It was located much further south in a warm tropical sea.

Billions upon billions of tiny shelled creatures – like small snails – were deposited on the floor of this tropical sea. In time they built up into rock, sometimes a thousand metres thick. Forces from beneath the sea pushed up the rocks and exposed them on the earth's surface. When the continents began to move apart, Ireland drifted northwards to its present location. The glaciers of the Ice Age scraped the Burren limestone clean of soil about 15,000 years ago, leaving it exposed to the winds and rains of the nearby Atlantic Ocean.

The poet John Betjeman wrote of the Burren:

*Stony seaboard, far and foreign,
Stony hills poured over space,
Stony outcrop of the Burren,
Stones in every fertile place ...*

General Ludlow, an officer in Oliver Cromwell's army in Ireland, said that the Burren had 'neither water enough to drown a man, nor a tree to hang him, nor soil enough to bury him.' What Ludlow might not have known was that the water of the Burren was mostly underground – in streams and rivers that had long since forced their way deep down under the limestone landscape.

Most streams disappear underground through 'swallow holes' which have been eroded in the limestone. As they make their way along underground, these streams often carve out splendid caves and caverns in the soft limestone. Rain water contains some carbon dioxide which turns it into a weak acid. This acid erodes or eats away the soft limestone rock. Even on the surface, the rocks of the Burren are being eroded about 1cm every 20 years. So the limestone that General Ludlow actually saw is not there at all today.

Kilfenora High Cross

TURLOUGHS

The limestone of the Burren has been eroded by the glaciers of the Ice Age, by the Atlantic winds and by the acid nature of the rains. The result is the spectacular Burren landscape. A fascinating feature of the Burren is its 'disappearing' lakes or turloughs.

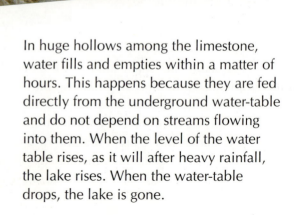

In huge hollows among the limestone, water fills and empties within a matter of hours. This happens because they are fed directly from the underground water-table and do not depend on streams flowing into them. When the level of the water table rises, as it will after heavy rainfall, the lake rises. When the water-table drops, the lake is gone.

QUESTIONS

1. Name the most common Irish rock.
2. What covers this rock over most of Ireland?
3. What does the word *Boireann* mean?
4. John Betjeman was a famous English poet who cycled through the Burren during the 1940s. Why do you think he described it as 'stony hills poured over space'?
5. In what county is the Burren?
6. How does rainfall help to erode the limestone?
7. The River Fergus flows on the surface for some distance in the Burren but then it disappears. Where do you think it goes?
8. What is a turlough?
9. Why does the water level rise and fall in a turlough?
10. Does the name of the place in which you live tell you anything about its Geography or its History?

orchid

FLORA AND FAUNA OF THE BURREN

The plant life of a particular area is called its flora. Just as the landscape of the Burren is extraordinary, the flora of this area is also amazing. For here in North Clare one can see plants growing side by side which would normally grow in two quite different parts of Europe. On the one hand there are plants from warm countries of the Mediterranean. There are also plants from the Arctic regions or the Alpine slopes.

How come that North meets South in the Burren? Botanists who study plants tell us that the plants of the Burren were not brought there by people. Most of them have been there for thousands of years. How they came there is something we do not quite fully understand.

The O'Brien Tower on the Cliffs of Moher

The Burren has a vast number of limestone blocks with deep cracks criss-crossing between them. Little can grow on the surface of the rock slabs themselves and this gives the landscape its bleak appearance. But in the cracks (called grykes) between the slabs, life is abundant.

The arctic and the southern plants produce millions of flowers during the spring and summer months. One of the best-known of these flowers is the blue Spring Gentian, which has been chosen as the symbol of the Burren. Small flat-growing trees and shrubs look as if they are afraid to push their heads up into the Atlantic winds. The hazel tree is very common among the Burren rocks.

Bell heather

Bee orchid

Foxglove

Rock-rose

Wild thyme

Spring gentian

Burnet rose

Where the growth is thick, one might be lucky enough to see a pine marten, fox, badger, stoat or red squirrel. Wild goats roam over the rocks, cropping off any grasses or shrubs that appear above ground level. On rainy evenings, armies of snails appear out of the grykes and crawl across the limestone slabs. One could count as many as seventy different kinds of snails on the Burren rocks.

Learn about your Irish landscape and how to enjoy it. You can begin with your local area and perhaps travel to a more distant landscape later in the year. Keep in mind one simple piece of advice:

'Take only photographs and leave behind only your footprints.'

John Buckley is a splendid modern Irish composer of classical music. One of his best-known compositions is *Boireann* – a piece which was written because John Buckley loves the Burren landscape.

'In my piece Boireann I have attempted to evoke the craggy, desolate beauty of the Burren. The outline of the stone, the special brilliance of the light, the extraordinary clarity of sound, the diverse and delicate shapes and colours of the flora all inspired me in composing the piece.' John Buckley

While we hope you enjoy learning about your world in *Worldwise*, we strongly suggest that you will also learn by going out to study landscapes. Some schools go on a day-tour to the Burren. If you go in the month of May you will see the flora of the Burren at their most beautiful.

Where in the world?

There have been many reports that spacecraft from other planets were seen in different parts of our own planet earth. To date we have no certain proof that we have been visited, but just for this lesson let's imagine ... a spaceship carrying friends from another galaxy has landed ... somewhere. Where? We simply are not sure at the moment. All we know is that the craft is in the Atlantic Ocean, west of Ireland. How can we help? How can we rescue these friendly beings? We can use a system called latitude and longitude to locate them and direct rescue services to them.

LATITUDE

Over 2,000 years ago the early Greeks developed a way of locating places on the surface of the earth. This is how they did it. If we take a large ball as the earth, we can draw a line around the middle. Can you remember the name we gave this line in *Worldwise 3*? Well done! We call it the equator. The equator divides the earth into the northern hemisphere and the southern hemisphere. The angles between the north pole and the equator are 90°. We can draw in other angles as well. When you examine your school globe you will see that all lines of latitude are parallel to the equator. They are often called parallels of latitude. The parallels north of the equator are in northern latitudes while those south of the equator are in southern latitudes.

In the tropics day-time changes to night-time very quickly

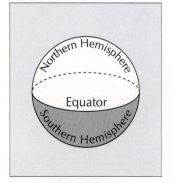

The equator is an imaginary line which divides the world into 2 half-spheres.

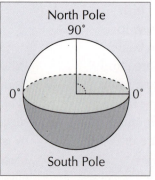

The angle between the equator and the North Pole is 90°.

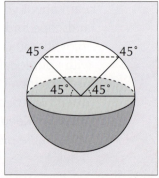

We can draw in other angles such as 45°.

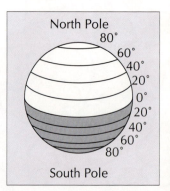

If we join up the points we make parallels of latitude.

QUESTIONS

1. The spacecraft from other planets which people claim to have seen are sometimes described as UFOs. What does this mean?
2. Name the race who first thought of latitude and longitude.
3. The line which divides the world into the northern hemisphere and the southern hemisphere is called the _____.
4. What are the angles between the south pole and the equator?
5. In *Worldwise 3* we had names for some special parallels of latitude. Write these names in their correct position on a drawing of the globe: the Tropic of Cancer (23½°N), the Tropic of Capricorn (23½°S), the Arctic Circle (66½°N) and the Antarctic Circle (66½°S).

LONGITUDE

It seems sensible that the equator (0°) is the half way line between the north pole and the south pole. An observatory called Greenwich in London is the starting point for dividing the world into east and west. Why Greenwich? There was no special reason but in 1884 it was agreed that 0° longitude would pass through Greenwich. This is called the prime meridian of longitude.

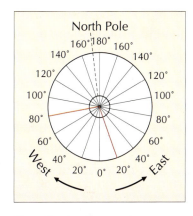

By going east or west we can measure from 0° to 180°. The line 180°W and the line 180°E are the same.

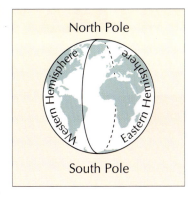

0° longitude is the prime meridian and it divides the world into 2 hemispheres.

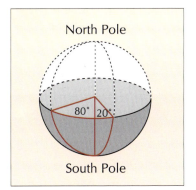

This shows how the lines 20°E and 80°W are marked out.

The prime meridian also divides the world into two – the eastern and western hemispheres. The eastern hemisphere is divided into 180 meridians (lines) of longitude, while the western hemisphere has exactly the same number. If two planes took off from London and one travelled east while the other travelled west at the same speed, at what line of longitude would they meet? They would meet at a meridian which is both 180° east and west! One last special point about meridians of longitude – they are all the same length and they all meet at the north pole and at the south pole.

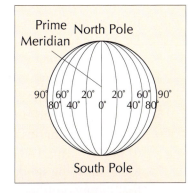

Meridians of longitude run from Pole to Pole. They are all equal in length.

QUESTIONS

1. What is the prime meridian and where would we find it?
2. The prime meridian divides the world into two hemispheres. Name them.
3. How many lines of longitude are there altogether? Hint – east plus west.
4. Where do meridians of longitude meet? Are they all the same length?
5. How are meridians of longitude different from parallels of latitude? Hint – what do parallel lines never do?

LATITUDE AND LONGITUDE

Here it is – the answer you've been waiting for! We can confirm that the visiting spaceship landed, briefly, in the Atlantic Ocean at 50°N and 20°W. This is how we describe the location of any place. These descriptions are called co-ordinates and we always give the latitude of a place first and its longitude second.

There is only one sad note in this chapter. By the time our rescue plane got to the correct co-ordinates, the spacecraft was just taking off and became one more .... unidentified flying object! Check in your atlas if the point 50°N, 20°W was anywhere near Ireland!

The Greenwich Meridian in London

QUESTIONS

1. In your atlas find the meridian of longitude at 20°E. Use a world map showing political units (countries). Start at the north pole and name each country you pass through until you reach the south pole.
2. Do the same exercise for 20°W. This is much easier as there are fewer countries.
3. Pick any other meridians you care to choose and repeat this exercise.
4. What countries would you pass through if you travelled east from the prime meridian along the parallel of latitude at 40°N?
5. Name the countries located on 40°S.
6. Name the countries you would find at the following co-ordinates: (80°N 40°W), (0° 60°W), (20°S 140°E), (20°N 80°E).
7. Make up some similar co-ordinate tests for your friends in class. Do remember that these co-ordinates refer only to parts of the countries. Large countries will pass through several degrees of latitude and longitude. Enjoy yourselves in finding more answers to the title of this chapter – where in the world?

3 Have you got the time please?

Children are often amazed to discover that while they are walking to school in the morning, other children in a different part of the world are walking home from school! To understand how this can happen, let us remind ourselves of some basic ideas we learned in *Worldwise 3*. The earth spins on its own axis once every day. While one half of the world is in light the other half is in darkness.

360° longitude = 24 hours
360° ÷ 24 = 1 hour
15° longitude = 1 hour

TIME

We can find out what time it is in any part of the world by doing a simple calculation. We know that it takes the earth 24 hours to turn on its axis. In this time it turns through 360° of longitude. 360 divided by 24 is 15. Therefore, for every 15 degrees we move from Greenwich, there is a time difference of one hour. We can see this quite clearly on our world map which shows time zones.

TIME ZONES

There are a several time zones in very large countries. Some time zones do not form perfect bands, because countries sometimes feel it is convenient to have the same time zone as their neighbours.

Ireland and Great Britain are in the same time zone.
Places in the same time zone share a time called standard time.
Ireland's standard time is called Greenwich Mean Time (GMT).

INTERNATIONAL DATE-LINE

Do you remember the meridian of longitude at which our planes heading east and west would meet? It was 180°E and W. This is called the common meridian. It is also called the International Date-Line because it is here that one date changes to another.

Depending on which direction we cross the date-line, we can gain or lose a day. If we go east we gain a day. On the other hand, we lose a day as we go west across the date-line.

When you leave home to go to school these Indian children are on their way home!

Around the World in Eighty Days

JULES VERNE

This book tells the story of Mr Phileas Fogg and his funny friend Passepartout, who set out to win a bet of £20,000 – a lot of money in 1872. Their timetable was as follows:

From London to Suez, by rail and steamboats	7 days
From Suez to Bombay, by steamer	13 days
From Bombay to Calcutta, by rail	3 days
From Calcutta to Hong Kong, by steamer	13 days
From Hong Kong to Yokohama (Japan), by steamer	6 days
From Yokohama to San Francisco by steamer	22 days
From San Francisco to New York, by rail	7 days
From New York to London, by steamer and rail	9 days
	80 days

When they arrived back in London they thought it had taken them 81 days to circle the globe but then they discovered that they had a day in hand. They were just in time to claim their winnings.

Can you explain how they made such a bad mistake in their calculations?

Could you plan out on a map the journey they took around the world in eighty days?

QUESTIONS

Study the time zone map on page 13 and answer these questions.
1 If it is 12 noon in Ireland what time is it in India? (Marked on the map as I).
2 What time is it in the eastern part of Brazil(B)?
3 What time is it in the western part of Australia(A)?
4 What time is it in Ethiopia(E)?
5 Look closely at the map and then fill in the missing words (earlier/later):
   (a) As we go east from Greenwich the time is _____ in the day.
   (b) As we go west from Greenwich the time is _____ in the day.
6 How many time zones has Canada?
7 Choose any other countries that interest you and ask your classmates some questions on them. If you feel really brave, why not change the time at Greenwich from 12 noon to another time?

TIME ZONES

Getting the balance right

We can identify three types of geographical environment. We have already looked at the first two in our *Worldwise* Series: the rural environment and the urban environment. The third type is called a primeval environment. This environment, still in its original state, allows us to go back, in a time-machine as it were, and look at part of the world before people began to change it.

THE AMAZING AMAZON

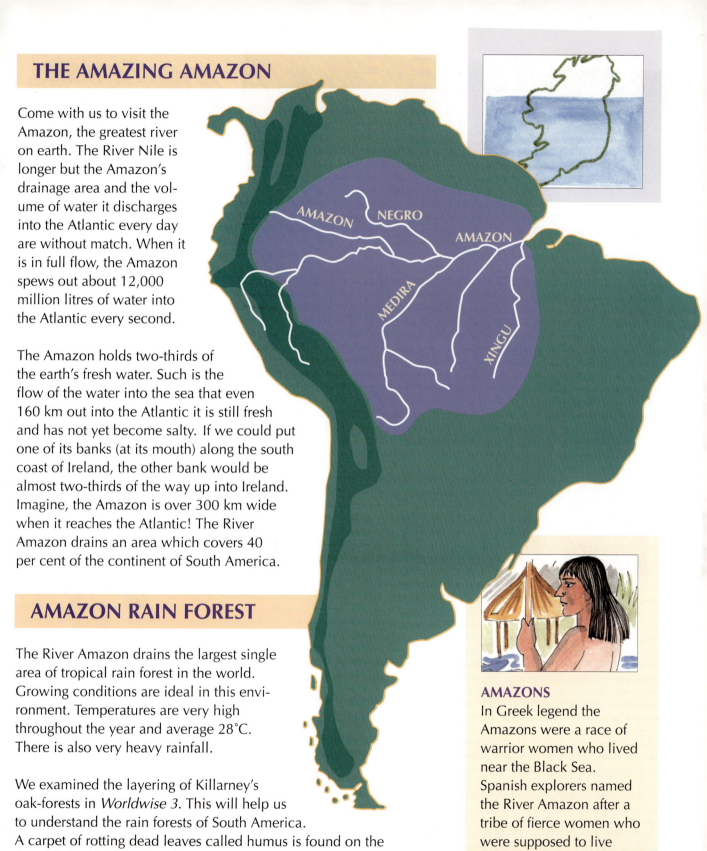

Come with us to visit the Amazon, the greatest river on earth. The River Nile is longer but the Amazon's drainage area and the volume of water it discharges into the Atlantic every day are without match. When it is in full flow, the Amazon spews out about 12,000 million litres of water into the Atlantic every second.

The Amazon holds two-thirds of the earth's fresh water. Such is the flow of the water into the sea that even 160 km out into the Atlantic it is still fresh and has not yet become salty. If we could put one of its banks (at its mouth) along the south coast of Ireland, the other bank would be almost two-thirds of the way up into Ireland. Imagine, the Amazon is over 300 km wide when it reaches the Atlantic! The River Amazon drains an area which covers 40 per cent of the continent of South America.

AMAZON RAIN FOREST

The River Amazon drains the largest single area of tropical rain forest in the world. Growing conditions are ideal in this environment. Temperatures are very high throughout the year and average 28°C. There is also very heavy rainfall.

We examined the layering of Killarney's oak-forests in *Worldwise 3*. This will help us to understand the rain forests of South America. A carpet of rotting dead leaves called humus is found on the forest floor. The light is very poor and the air is damp and humid. It is home to thousands of insects and some ground-dwelling animals like the tapir and the jaguar.

AMAZONS
In Greek legend the Amazons were a race of warrior women who lived near the Black Sea. Spanish explorers named the River Amazon after a tribe of fierce women who were supposed to live along its banks.

The Brazilian rain forest being cleared for plantation agriculture

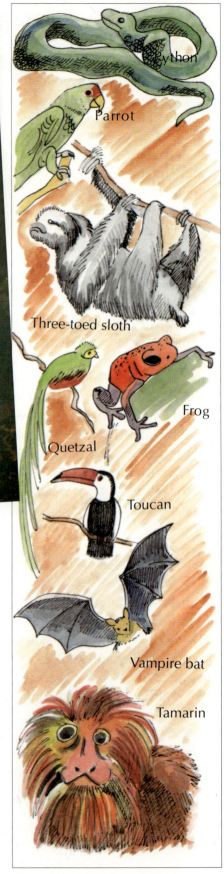

The forest canopy grows up to 40 metres high and this is the ceiling which blocks out the light. We find most of the forest life in the canopy. Scientists have suggested that up to one million species of animal and plant life, or nearly two-thirds of the total known on earth, are found in the Amazonian rain forest. The canopy is alive with colour and sound. Brightly-coloured parrots and macaws fill the air with their screeching. Toucans and hummingbirds flit in and out among the branches. The lazy sloth just hangs there, half asleep, while spider and howler monkeys swing furiously from tree to tree. There are only a few of the gorgeous golden tamarin left. Amid all the noise of the rain forest snakes of many colours and sizes slide noiselessly along the branches. Yet this fabulous wildlife environment, which took millions of years to develop, is being destroyed at an alarming rate.

QUESTIONS

1. Which is the longest river in the world?
2. Why, do you think, are there no rain forests along its banks?
3. The Amazon is about 6,500 km long. What country does it mostly flow through?
4. Is it far from the equator?
5. In which layer of the rainforest does its teeming life exist?
6. How many species of flora and fauna are found in the Amazonian rain forest?
7. Which is your favourite bird of the rain forest? Draw and colour it.
8. Which is your favourite animal of the rain forest?
9. How did the howler monkey get its name? (Hint: It can make its call louder by inflating a little skin bag under its chin.)
10. The spider monkey has a prehensile tail. Find out what that means.

EXPLOITING THE AMAZON

The native people of the rain forest are Indians. They have a life-style that has changed little over many centuries. Their food comes mainly from fishing and hunting. They clear only small areas of forest at a time and move on to a new patch when the soil becomes poor. The small patches they do clear are quickly reclaimed by the forest.

From 1960 onwards roads were built into the rain forest and Amazonia was opened up to many new settlers. These settlers found minerals such as copper, manganese, nickel, silver, tin, gold, bauxite and iron. Worse still, they began to clear large forest areas to make huge cattle ranches. Every year now, a forest area the size of Belgium is deliberately destroyed by fire.

The clearance of these large forest areas allows the heavy tropical rains to wash away the soil. The Amazon River deposits vast amounts of soil in the Atlantic but what use is it there? Many of the world's precious hardwood trees, such as mahogany, are destroyed. These trees take between 60 and 100 years to mature.

Many Indians have been murdered by new settlers who are searching for minerals and land. Thousands of species of plants and animals, which could have been of great value in science and medicine, have been destroyed forever.

THE FUTURE OF AMAZONIA

Cattle are reared on many of the ranches made on the cleared land. These cattle are used to make hamburgers – especially for the American market. It takes a forest clearance of about the size of a small kitchen to produce a single hamburger. This piece of land would have supported one single big tree, about 50 saplings and seedlings of some 20-30 species. And these are now burned and gone – forever. Almost half of the world's rain forests have already been destroyed.

Efforts have already begun to preserve the Amazonian rain forest. Developed countries should not tell developing countries like Brazil how to treat the environment. Instead, they should lead by example and offer terms of trade which are fair. People in Amazonia must be helped, with financial aid if necessary, to realise that our world is one vast environment. Its future belongs to us all.

QUESTIONS

1. Cattle ranching in Amazonia creates few jobs. Who, do you think, makes most profit out of it?
2. How could extensive mining and forest clearance damage this precious environment?
3. One head of cattle needs 1 hectare of grazing land the year after the forest has been cleared. After 10 years it needs 7 hectares. Why is this?
4. There were once about 10 million native Indians of the Amazon. Now there are only a few thousand. Who lives best in harmony with the rain forest, them or new settlers?
5. Suggest some ways in which Irish people can help to save the Amazonian rain forest and get the balance between development and conservation right.

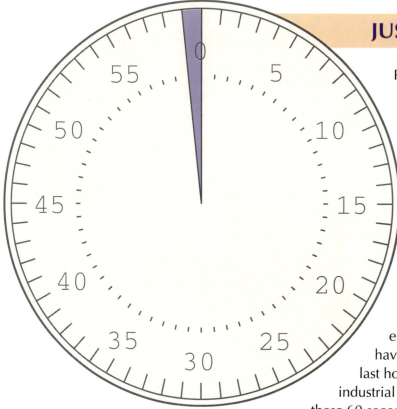

JUST A MINUTE!

Planet earth is 4,600 million years old. To simplify matters we can liken the earth to a person of 46 years of age. Nothing is known about the first 7 years of this person's life. Little is known of the middle period and only at the age of 42 did the earth begin to flower. Dinosaurs did not appear until one year ago, when the planet was 45 years of age. Mammals arrived only 8 months ago; in the middle of last week human-like apes evolved into humans and at the weekend the last ice-age enveloped the earth. Modern humans have been around for 4 hours. During the last hour, humans discovered agriculture. The industrial revolution began a minute ago. During these 60 seconds of biological time, we have turned our planet earth into a rubbish tip!

THE ENVIRONMENT GAME

We all need to be aware of special places and issues like Amazonia. The future of many animal and plant species depends on people who care about their world. To help you understand your world a little better, we have a special game for you to play.

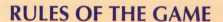

RULES OF THE GAME

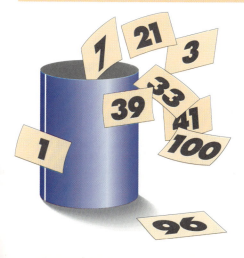

The aim of the Environment Game is to cause as little damage as possible to the environment. To play you need 100 small squares of paper, number 1 to 100. You can use cloakroom tickets if you wish. Put all 100 numbers into a container and mix them well. Up to five players can take part. Numbers are drawn out in turn by the players until the container is empty. Players incur one penalty point for the numbers shown on the map. The player with the least number of penalites at the end wins the game. Greenpeace can help you. If you draw one of their five numbers you get credit for two penalty points.

THE ENVIRONMENT GAME

12 St Lawrence River: Whales found with more than 30 dangerous chemicals in their body tissues

16 Mississippi Corridor: 2,000 tonnes of chemical waste into the atmosphere every year

70 Newfoundland, Canada: Greenpeace stops slaughter of seal pups

50 Aleutian Islands, USA: Greenpeace stops atomic bomb tests

56 Rocky Mountains, USA: Californian condor is endangered

26 New Mexico, USA: American bald eagle facing extinction

24 Mediterranean coast: Health hazards in holiday resorts on the 'concrete coast'

9 Atlantic Ocean: Greenpeace achieves a European Ban on the burning of toxic waste at sea

30 Pacific: Greenpeace stops slaughter of whales

8 Eastern Pacific: Slaughter of dolphins by fishing crews

68 Gabon: Mountain gorilla facing extinction

32 West Africa: Dumping of toxic waste from some European countries

37 Mururoa Atoll, Pacific: More than 130 French nuclear tests held here

60 Tanzania: faces extinction

4 Brazil: Destruction of rain forests

40 South Atlantic: Slaughter of whales continues despite international

20 Antarctica: Last unspoiled continent threatened by oil and mineral exploration

GLOBAL ACTION MAKES OUR WORLD GO ROUND

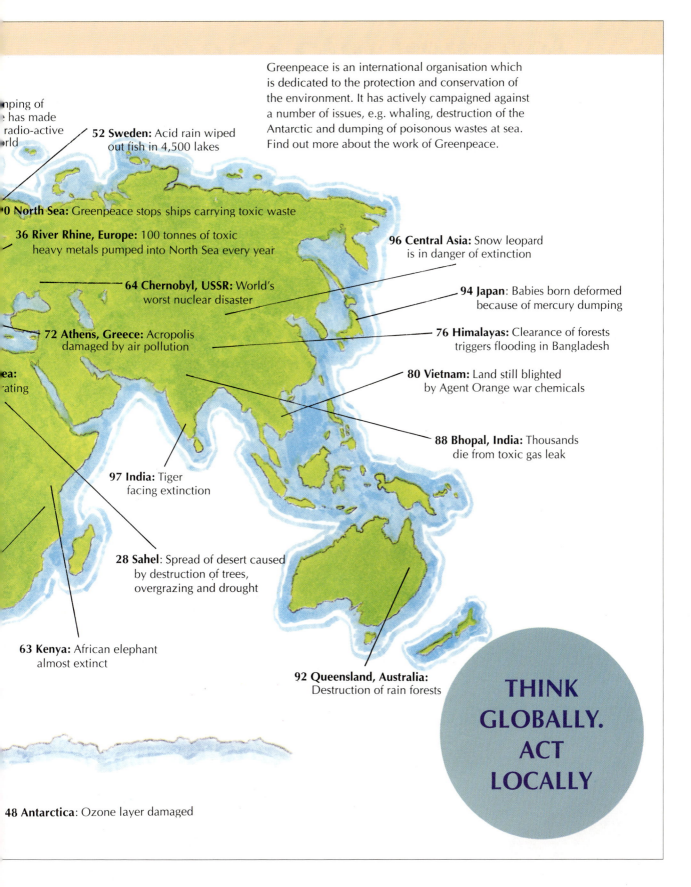

Greenpeace is an international organisation which is dedicated to the protection and conservation of the environment. It has actively campaigned against a number of issues, e.g. whaling, destruction of the Antarctic and dumping of poisonous wastes at sea. Find out more about the work of Greenpeace.

52 Sweden: Acid rain wiped out fish in 4,500 lakes

0 North Sea: Greenpeace stops ships carrying toxic waste

36 River Rhine, Europe: 100 tonnes of toxic heavy metals pumped into North Sea every year

64 Chernobyl, USSR: World's worst nuclear disaster

72 Athens, Greece: Acropolis damaged by air pollution

96 Central Asia: Snow leopard is in danger of extinction

94 Japan: Babies born deformed because of mercury dumping

76 Himalayas: Clearance of forests triggers flooding in Bangladesh

80 Vietnam: Land still blighted by Agent Orange war chemicals

88 Bhopal, India: Thousands die from toxic gas leak

97 India: Tiger facing extinction

28 Sahel: Spread of desert caused by destruction of trees, overgrazing and drought

63 Kenya: African elephant almost extinct

92 Queensland, Australia: Destruction of rain forests

48 Antarctica: Ozone layer damaged

THINK GLOBALLY. ACT LOCALLY

# Journey into space

Today we are travelling out into space. Climb aboard our spaceship – it is named *Spacewise 1*. Fasten your seat-belts and off we go to view our planet earth from a distance. We will need to travel at a speed of 40,000km per hour to break free of the force of gravity – otherwise our spaceship would come crashing back to earth. If our speed is too great we would fly off out into the darkness of space. Don't worry, we can control the speed of *Spacewise 1* and all will be well.

PLANET EARTH

This is what planet earth looks like from our position out in space. Most of the land is in the northern hemisphere. We can recognise the shapes of the great land masses and oceans. Nearly ¾ of the earth's surface is covered with water.

Looking through the window of *Spacewise 1* we can see that only half the earth is lit up by sunlight. The other half is in darkness or shadow. We say that the sun 'rises' in the east and 'sinks' in the west. This is because we must look east in the morning to see the first rays of sunlight coming. The sun is not moving relative to the earth. In fact it is the earth that spins on its own axis and orbits around the sun.

GLOBES

Sunrise and sunset are a little difficult to understand. One of the easiest ways to illustrate sunrise and sunset is to spin a globe on its axis while holding a torch in a fixed position. This really helps us to see that it is the earth and not the sun which is moving.

THE SEASONS

The earth's axis is not perpendicular (straight up). The planet is inclined at an angle as it spins in space. This tilting of the earth gives us the seasons. As it travels, the tilt of its axis is always in the same direction. If the earth's axis was not tilted at an angle, our weather would be the same all year round. In June the northern hemisphere where we live is tilted towards the sun. Because of this the sun shines more directly on the northern hemisphere than on the southern hemisphere. As a result we have summer weather while it is winter in Australia and New Zealand. When they have summer, we have our winter.

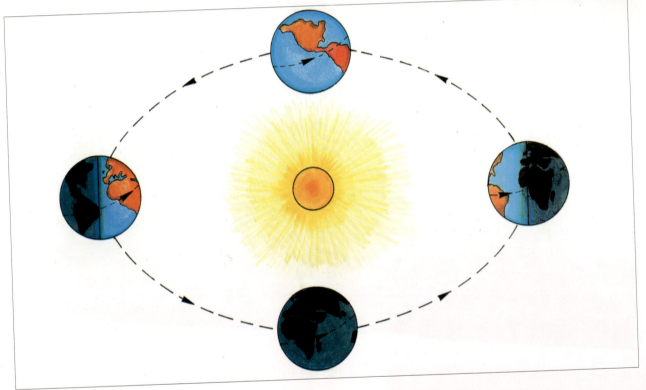

Countries on or near the equator are not affected by the tilting of the earth and so they do not have four different seasons like we do. They also have days and nights of twelve hours each, all year round. On the other hand, the places on earth most affected are the areas around the poles. So in the far northern countries, such as Norway, there is daylight for almost 24 hours in summer and this goes on for six months. While this is happening there are six months of darkness at the Antarctic.

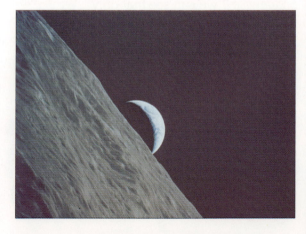

For Your Consideration!

The Latin word for star is *sidus* and the word 'consider' literally means 'to observe the stars'!

1. What would happen in your classroom if the force of gravity could magically be turned off?
2. Where in the world is The Land of the Midnight Sun?
3. Why do we have leap years? When will the next leap year be? What is the extra date added in a leap year?
4. The shortest day of the year is called the winter solstice. This means the sun is taking a rest. What is the shortest day of the year in Ireland? How many hours of daylight do we have on that day?
5. When is the summer solstice, therefore? What happens on that day? Is solstice a good word for what actually happens?
6. It is not only planet earth that has a force of gravity. All the bodies in space have gravity. The force of gravity of the sun keeps the earth moving around in its annual orbit. Try to find out a little more about the man whose name is strongly connected with the discovery of the laws of gravity. (Hint – weNotn!)

THE MOON

Now back to our spaceship. Can you see that small body orbiting around the earth? That's our moon of course. You've often heard of the light of the moon. Well there's no such thing. The moon has no light of its own. It merely reflects the light of the sun back onto earth. People say the moon looks like a human face. This is because there are hills and valleys on the moon and the light of the sun casts shadows on the lunar surface.

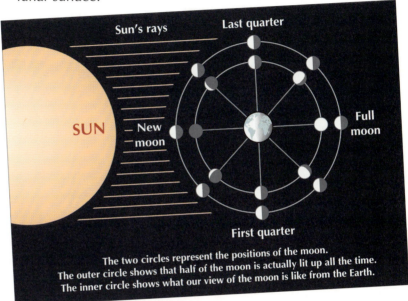

The two circles represent the positions of the moon. The outer circle shows that half of the moon is actually lit up all the time. The inner circle shows what our view of the moon is like from the Earth.

MOONWALKING

Astronauts have landed on the moon. The first moon landings were made in 1969. The journey from earth to the moon is as long as going around the earth about 10 times. In size the earth is 50 times larger than the moon.

Have you noticed that the moon appears to take on different shapes, ranging from a narrow crescent to a full circle. This is because we see different parts of the half of the moon that is being lit up by sunlight. These different shapes are called 'phases of the moon'.

When the moon is directly between the earth and the sun we cannot see any of the lit-up half at all and we call it a new moon – it looks quite dark in fact. But when the earth is directly between the moon and the sun we can see all the lit-up half. This is a full moon. We can see a half moon when it is a quarter or three-quarters way round on its orbit.

ECLIPSES

An eclipse occurs when the sun's light is blocked by either the earth or the moon. This does not happen very frequently. Eclipses, therefore, were a source of wonder, even fear, to people long ago.

When the earth passes between the sun and the moon its shadow is cast over the surface of the moon. This is a lunar eclipse.

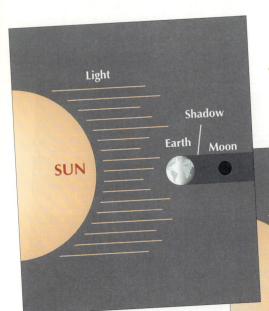

A solar eclipse occurs when the moon passes between the earth and the sun. Sunlight over part of the earth is blotted out by the moon.

THE SOLAR SYSTEM

Our earth, with its moon and the sun around which they both travel, are parts of what is called the solar system. The sun is at the centre of the solar system and is the only source of light and heat for the entire system. Because it gives out light and heat we say the sun is a star. Earth is one of the nine planets that orbit the sun and these with other bodies – such as moons, meteors, asteroids and comets – make up the solar system.

In the drawing of the solar system on p.27 the planets and their moons are drawn to scale so that you can compare their sizes. Why did we not draw the full picture of the sun? When you realise that the sun makes up over 99 per cent of the mass of the solar system, you begin to understand how very small planet earth really is.

To Do

1. Write the names of the nine planets of the solar system, starting with the planet nearest to the sun.
2. Is the moon a planet? (A planet orbits around a star and is heated and lit by that star.)
3. Which seems to be the largest of the planets?
4. Which is the smallest of the planets?
5. Three of the planets have rings around them. These rings are made of small pieces of rock and ice. Name the three ringed planets.
6. An asteroid is a piece of rock floating in space. Which two planets have a belt of thousands of asteroids between them?

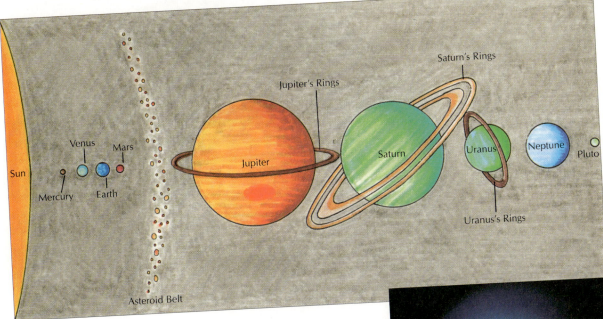

THE MILKY WAY

Just as planet earth is only a tiny part of the solar system, the solar system itself is only a tiny part of the milky way. The milky way is a galaxy or group of stars, of which the sun is just one. Our sun is indeed quite an ordinary star, quite like any of the other hundred thousand million stars that make up the milky way. You can see many of them sparkling and twinkling in the night sky. The milky way is shaped rather like a spinning firework. We call it a spiral-shaped galaxy. Our solar system is not at the centre of the milky way but much nearer to the rim of the fiery wheel. This wheel takes 225 million earth years to spin once in space.

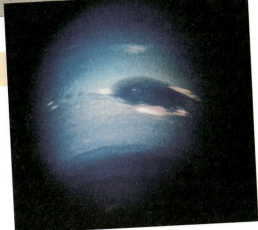

Neptune, viewed form *Voyager 2*

Mars, viewed from *Viking 1*

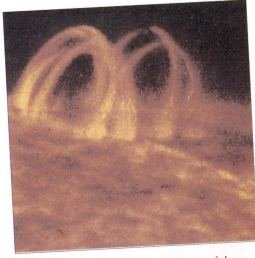

Flares dance high from the surface of the sun

THE UNIVERSE

Aren't the distances and the time spans in space amazing? Can you take any more? Just as the earth is a tiny part of the solar system and this is only a tiny part of the milky way, our galaxy in turn is only a tiny part of the known universe. Breath-taking, isn't it? There are some hundred thousand million galaxies in the universe. Some of them are spiral-shaped like ours, some are oval, others are round. They are all very far away from each other. We measure such distances in light-years. A light-year is the distance light would travel in a full year – and light travels at a speed of 300,000 kilometres per second. The nearest galaxy to the milky way is about two million light years away. And the galaxies are moving farther away from each other all the time.

The Andromeda galaxy

DOWN TO EARTH

Spacewise 1 is returning to earth. Tiny as it is, our planet is the only part of the universe that we know for sure has life on it. There is no life on the moon – people have been there to see. The solar heat is too severe on any of the planets nearer to the sun to allow life as we know it to exist. On the planets which are further away from the sun than we are, conditions are too cold to sustain life. We just don't know what it is like in most parts of the universe. Our little planet is precious, so let's mind it – for Heaven's sake!

6 Up with people

About 10,000 years ago, a great change took place in the way people lived. They no longer depended on hunting and food-gathering in order to survive. They became farmers. Before this Agricultural Revolution took place there were no more than 10 million people in the world.

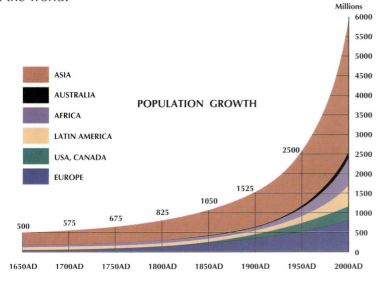

By the time of Christ the population had grown to 250 million. It took 1,500 more years for this figure to grow to 500 million. Then it took only 350 years for the number to double once more to a billion (1,000 million). This increased rate of population growth was caused by the Industrial Revolution that you read about in *Worldwise 2*.

There were 2 billion people on planet earth by 1930. The population of the world reached 5 billion in 1987 and it is estimated that by the year 2000 AD the figure will reach 6 billion people. This recent rapid growth is called the population explosion.

For most of human history, disease, famine and warfare have often reduced the world's population. In the fourteenth century the Black Death wiped out about one third of Europe's population. There were 8 million people in Ireland before the Great Famine. One million died during the famine years and another five million left Ireland between 1850 and 1910 to seek a better life in Britain or in America. About 70 million Europeans lost their lives during the Second World War.

We will examine the reasons for population increase on page 30.

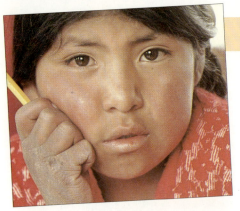

PROGRESS IN MEDICINE AND HEALTH CARE

New cures and treatments have been discovered that help people to live longer than before. In earlier times many, many children died at birth or in early infancy. In 1950 the average life-expectancy of people throughout the world was 47 years. Now it averages about 63 years. In developed countries average life expectancy is up to 75 years while in less developed countries it is often as low as 45 years.

BETTER FARMING TECHNIQUES

Famine often resulted from crop failure. While there are still famines in our world today, better methods of providing water and better control of crop diseases generally mean healthier crops and animals.

IMPROVED COMMUNICATIONS

In former times plagues and famines could happen in remote places, unknown to the world outside. Today, improved communications through radio, telephone and television enable us to learn quickly about people in need. Even now, one of the greatest problems is the difficulty of getting supplies quickly to the places where help is most needed.

QUESTIONS

1. When did the Agricultural Revolution take place?
2. When was the Industrial Revolution?
3. What is the present population of the world? You can add on about 80 million people for every year on to the 5 billion of 1987.
4. When did the Black Death sweep across Europe? Do you know what caused it to spread?
5. When was the Great Famine in Ireland? Do you know what caused it?
   Are there any stories about it in your own area?
6. When was World War 1 fought? Where did most of the fighting take place? How did it end?
7. How long did World War 2 last? How did it end?
8. Make a list of Relief Organisations that help to distribute food and supplies to famine areas.
9. What is the average life expectancy in the world today?
10. Why do people in developed countries have a longer life expectancy than people in less developed countries?

Environmental damage in Bangladesh

THE WORLD'S PEOPLE

The population of the world is not spread out evenly across the globe. Many areas of the earth are not suitable for humans at all. Other regions are very thickly populated. Nobody at all can live in the very frozen wastes of the Arctic or the Antarctic. The cold tundra of North America, northern Europe and northern Asia are home to the few Eskimoes and Lapps who live there. These people live by fishing, hunting and following their reindeer herds. The hot desert regions of the world do not naturally yield any kind of crops and are difficult environments in which to live.

AREAS OF POPULATION DENSITY

Some areas of the earth are very densely populated. For example, over half the people of our world are crowded together in the monsoon lands of south-east Asia. The many millions of people who live there depend on the monsoon rains and on the fertile lands of the region to provide them with enough food.

When famines, storms, floods or earthquakes strike this part of the world, the damage can be enormous. Of the countries in this part of the world, only Japan is highly industrialised. There are also several countries in this region which are called newly industrialised countries (NICs). Singapore and South Korea are two examples.

Shanty developments in Brazil

THE GROWTH OF CITIES

At the beginning of the twentieth century there were 11 'millionaire' cities in the world. In the early 1960s there were more than 100. By the end of this century 60 per cent of the world's population will live in cities. New towns and cities are being built all the time. Cities in the developing world are growing faster than those in the developed world.

DENSITY OF POPULATION

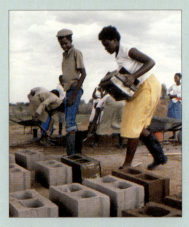

Africa's urban population is growing very quickly.

Both the Republic of Ireland and Libya have a population of about 3.5 million people. Because Libya is twenty-five times larger than Ireland, it follows that the population of Libya is much more thinly spread than ours. Put another way, we can say that Ireland has a higher density of population than Libya. You can see that in the table on the bottom of this page.

If we divide the population of a country by its area, we can work out the density of population in that country. In this way we can compare the density of population in one country with the density of population in another.

Largest Cities

Population experts suggest that by the year 2000 AD the largest cities in the world will be:

1	Mexico City	31m
2	Sao Paulo	25m
3	Tokyo	24m
4	Shanghai	24m
5	New York	22m
6	Peking	20m
7	Rio de Janeiro	19m
8	Calcutta	16m
9	Bombay	16m
10	Los Angeles	14m
11	Seoul	14m

Where in the world are these cities? Use your atlas if you need some help.

Population Density

	IRELAND	LIBYA	PUERTO RICO
POPULATION:	3.5m	3.6m	3.6m
AREA (SQ KM):	70,000	1,760,000	9,000
DENSITY (PER SQ KM):	$\frac{3,500,000}{70,000} = 50$	$\frac{3,600,000}{1,760,000} = 2$	$\frac{3,600,000}{9,000} = 400$

WORLD POPULATION DENSITY

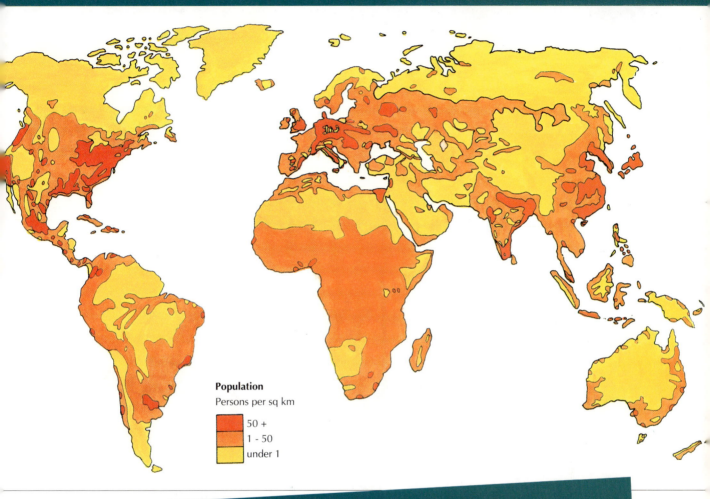

Population
Persons per sq km
- 50 +
- 1 - 50
- under 1

TO DO

This map of the world shows the areas of greatest and least density of population.
The various colours represent the number of persons per sq km.

1. List some areas of the world with a high density of population.
2. In each case suggest a reason why this might be so.
3. List some areas of the world with a very low density of population.
4. In each case suggest a reason for this.
5. Compare population density in the northern hemisphere with that in the southern hemisphere.
6. Where is Libya?
7. Why do you think that Libya has a much lower density of population than Ireland?
8. Where is Puerto Rico?
9. How many times greater than our density is that of Puerto Rico?
10. Can you suggest a reason why this is so?

# On the streets where you live

As countries develop they change from being very agricultural to a mixture of agriculture and other industries. More and more people live in villages, towns and cities. These urban living places are often called central places. They provide many services both for the people who live in them and for the people in the countryside who travel to them.

SERVICES

The services which are offered by central places are divided into lower-order and higher-order groups. Lower-order items such as milk or bread are available in even the smallest villages. Higher-order services, such as those offered by doctors or solicitors, tend to be available in larger towns and cities. This gives us a very useful rule – the larger the urban centre, the greater the number of services it offers to people.

TO DO

1. What modern method of transport has changed the distances over which people can travel for services? Can you explain why this is so?
2. Explain the rule – the larger the urban centre, the greater the number of services it offers to people.
3. Why are higher-order services usually concentrated in larger towns and cities?
4. Can you suggest why lower-order items such as newspapers are available in even the smallest villages?
5. Use your atlas to look at the distribution of villages, towns and cities in your own county.

LOOKING AT IRISH TOWNS

It is also very important that we look at the shape and colours of our towns. The word fabric is used to describe the make-up of villages, towns and cities. It describes how they look and how they feel. Generally speaking, the people who built our towns had a 'very good eye'. What do we mean by this?

Most Irish towns have streets that are lined with buildings which are usually of the same height and are joined directly to each other. The same types of building materials were used and one can see the same kind of decoration and colouring all along the street. This gives a great sense of unity to the streetscape. The results are usually very pleasing to the eye.

There are often shops on the ground floor of the buildings and the shop-owners and their families live in the rooms overhead. If any houses were built taller than the others, they would probably be the houses in the town centre — giving to that area an air of dignity which it deserved.

Important public buildings such as churches and market-houses might also be located in the town centre. Overall, Irish towns have remained pleasant and safe places in which to live.

URBAN SPRAWL

From the 1960s onwards, towns began to expand and develop very quickly. Our towns are now centres of industry – places where products and goods are made and despatched for sale. These recent developments have created many problems. Much of our modern urban growth has been along the roadways that lead into the town.

New houses, often bungalows, line both sides of the roads. Though lovely in themselves, they are very different in design and materials from the traditional town houses of earlier centuries. Neither is there any unity of style among the new houses themselves – every builder seems to have followed his or her own taste.

The result is that the approaches to our towns often suffer from this rather tasteless development which we call 'urban sprawl'. There is no order in the development. There is no clear sense of where the country ends and the town begins.

TOWN APPROACHES

As we approach a distant town, the first glimpses we get of it are the spires and steeples of its churches. The churches are often built on high ground, surrounded by trees and railings. Getting nearer to the town, we have a feeling of anticipation about what lies ahead. And if there is a bend on the road as it enters the town, our curiosity increases still more.

What lies beyond this bend? Traffic is forced to slow down on the bend, preventing cars from speeding into the town. In modern times, with increased traffic on the roads, these bends are often removed and replaced with wide carriageways. What about the petrol stations? Do they always fit in with our idea of good taste? What about the large, unsightly advertisements that line the road on both sides, overshadowing even the traffic signs? Would it not be so much nicer to enter our towns between well-kept hedgegrows or lines of flowering shrubs?

TOWN CENTRES

The centre of a town is always special. Sometimes we know we have arrived there when we find ourselves in a broad open space like a square or a fair-green. The town square may well have been the commercial centre of the town in days gone by. It was there, perhaps, that fairs and markets were held. Circuses and travelling shows pitched their tents there overnight. Nowadays most cattle are sold in indoor marts. Travelling shows are fewer than before. The old original buildings of the town centre cannot last forever. Some of them have to be rebuilt or replaced.

Problems often arise when a modern building is built into a streetscape which is old in character. New buildings must respect the overall pattern of the existing street design. That is not to say that new buildings should always be copies of older ones being replaced, or that the old ones should be rebuilt as originally were.

The old Shee Almhouse in Kilkenny, now a modern tourist office

The requirements of modern trading make their own demands on buildings and this has to be taken into account. New buildings should respect the height of the rest of the streetscape and they should use materials and colours that are not out of place among older neighbours. High buildings can cause problems – they can dominate the skyline and upset the balance of the streetscape that has grown up over a long time.

TO DO

Look closely at the village, town or city in which you live. If you live in the countryside look at the centre closest to you. Begin by making a list of the services which are available in your town. Examine the types of buildings – their heights, colours, materials, etc. Make sketches of special buildings which are of historical, geographical or architectural interest. Get to know your town really well because it is through understanding it that we can truly appreciate it.

8 Weatherwatch

HERE IS THE FORECAST

The science of weather forecasting plays a vital role in the lives of many people. The decision on whether or not to put to sea in a fishing boat should be based on an accurate weather forecast. Pilots planning an air route from one city to another need to know the weather conditions along the way. Farmers need precise information about frost, rain, wind and several other weather processes.

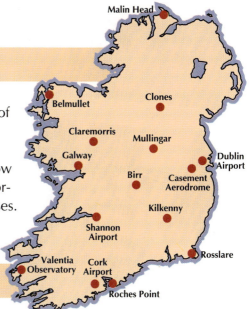

Ireland's weather stations

THE METEOROLOGICAL SERVICE

People depend on the information supplied by the women and men who work in the Meteorological Service. The Irish part of the World Meteorological Organisation began its work in 1936. Today, it is a scientific source of information about the weather.

WEATHER STATIONS

The 15 weather stations which are located around Ireland are staffed every day of the year. Weather doesn't take a break, so it is important that up-to-date information is constantly available. Every hour of the day, the people who work in these stations measure the weather. They make more detailed measurements every six hours.

Ireland's constantly changing weather!

THE MET HEADQUARTERS

All this information is transmitted to the Irish Meteorological Headquarters at Glasnevin in Dublin. There it is entered into the computer system and then plotted onto a weather chart.

The data is recorded.

The data is received in Glasnevin.

The memory section of the weather analysis in Glasnevin

Analysis of the weather charts

Weather Charts

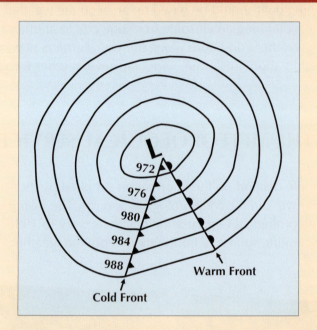

Fronts are the lines along which different air masses meet. Weather forecasters use symbols on their charts to identify warm and cold fronts.

Weather charts show air pressure readings at sea level. Places of equal pressure are joined together by lines called isobars. An area of high pressure is shown on the weather map by the letter H. It is a sign of good weather. The letter L stands for an area of low pressure and this can mean that rain is on the way. Look out for the weather forecast on television and see if Ireland is coming under high or low pressure. Look out too for cold fronts and warm fronts.

QUESTIONS

1. Name some groups of people who depend on accurate weather forecasts.
2. The oldest Irish weather station was established in 1866 at Valentia, Co. Kerry. Can you explain why it was built in this part of Ireland? Hint – Transatlantic!
3. Try to explain why the 15 weather stations are located where they are.
4. The first (of four) detailed weather observations is made at midnight every day. When are the other three observations made?
5. Put the main steps in preparing a complete weather chart into a flow diagram.

   OBSERVATION TRANSMISSION ⟩ ⟩

6. Describe briefly what you might find attractive about working in one of the 15 Irish weather stations.
7. What aspects might you find less attractive?
8. What kind of weather comes with high pressure?
9. How is this shown on a map?
10. What are weather fronts?

WEATHER FORECASTS

The weather observations made in Ireland are also sent to other meteorological services, particularly those in Western Europe. We also receive information from other sources.

This information from other countries is used by Irish forecasters. The data from land stations in other countries and from weather ships is plotted onto charts. Extra knowledge is provided by studying satellite photographs and radiosonde information from balloons about the upper atmosphere.

The forecasters use charts to build up a picture of what was happening when the weather was last observed. They can also accurately predict or forecast what is most likely to happen over the following few hours or even days. They use their professional training and computer programmes to guide them in making forecasts. It is quite likely that weather forecasts in the future will be able to predict weather several weeks in advance by using new computer technology.

Satellites

Land stations in other countries

Weather ships

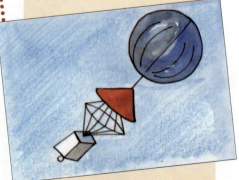

Weather balloons

Joan Blackburn, television forecast

Evelyn Murphy: weather query by telephone

Weather forecasts are made available to the public in a number of ways. Given the sheer size of our atmosphere and the fact that Ireland is located in a very changeable weather zone, the men and women of the Irish Meteorological Service do a really remarkable job.

Liam Keegan: forecast on radio

QUESTIONS

1. Why might information about the Irish weather be very useful to countries in Western Europe?
2. Suggest some reasons why satellite images are so useful in weather analysis and forecasting.
3. There are four sources for weather forecasts shown in our photographs. What special advantages does each of them have?
4. The automatic phone service which provides a weather forecast is available 24 hours a day. Find in the Golden Pages under 'Weather Forcasts' what number you should ring to get the weather forecast for your area.
5. Get a forecast for tomorrow's weather. Check during the day how accurate the forecast is. You can make notes if you wish and discuss then in class during your next Geography lesson.

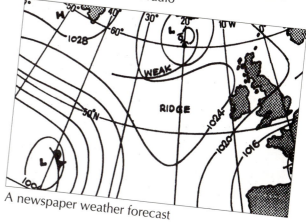
A newspaper weather forecast

 # Wonders of the natural world

There is a very real danger as the countries of the world become more developed. People may become so caught up in the rush that they stop looking around them. They may no longer notice the beauty and wonders of their natural world. There is one wonder that everyone can notice nearly every day. It is the majesty of clouds.

CLOUDS

The atmosphere contains considerable amounts of water vapour. This water vapour is constantly rising from the land and oceans by evaporation. Before it actually falls again as rain, it is suspended (held) in the atmosphere. We see this water vapour as clouds when it is cooled high above the ground. Some clouds which are visible very high in the atmosphere are made of specks of ice and have a lovely white colour.

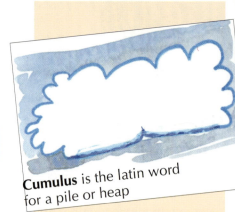

Cumulus is the latin word for a pile or heap

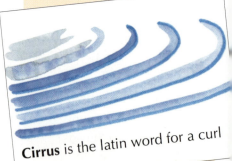

Cirrus is the latin word for a curl

TYPES OF CLOUDS

No, contrary to what some people think, clouds are not all the same. In 1803, an English meteorologist called Luke Howard suggested a way of putting clouds into groups. He said that there were three basic cloud shapes and he used Latin names to describe them. His groups are still used today. The next time you look at a really cloudy sky try to decide which of Howard's groups best describe the clouds you can see.

Stratus is the latin word for a layer or a band

These are the three main types of cloud.

44

LIGHTNING AND THUNDER

One cloud type is very capable of being a real trouble-maker! It is called *cumulonimbus* or the thundercloud. Inside *cumulonimbus* clouds the air is moving upwards in a violent fashion. The uplift of air prevents raindrops from falling down to earth. Scientists are not sure exactly how it happens, but electrical energy is generated by the raindrops and ice crystals bumping together in the strong current of air.

The clouds become charged with electricity. A positive charge gathers at the top of the cloud. A negative charge gathers at the bottom. This build-up of different electrical charges is the cause of lightning and thunder.

The negative charge at the base of the cloud causes a positive build-up on the ground. When the build-up reaches a certain strength some of the negative charge leaps off towards the ground. This creates a path through the air and a much stronger positive current charges up along the path from the ground. This release of electricity is the flash of lightning we see.

The air all around the flash of lightning expands with a bang. This is the thunder we hear. We should understand that lightning travels at the speed of light, which is much faster than the speed of sound. So which do we notice first? Yes, the lightning is seen first.

The farther away from us the lightning storm is, the longer the gap between the lightning and the thunder. Only if the thunderstorm is just overhead will there be little or no gap between the lightning and the thunder.

DANGER
Try to remain indoors during a thunderstorm. Remember lightning can kill.

To find out how far away a thunderstorm is, count the seconds between when you see the flash of lightning and hear the thunder. Divide the time by 8 and you will know the distance of the storm from you in kilometres.

QUESTIONS

1. Clouds may be made of specks of_____ or specks of _____.
2. Luke Howard used three Latin words to describe the basic cloud shapes. What are they and what do they mean?
3. Can you name any other types of cloud?
4. Name the cloud which is very capable of being a troublemaker. Why is this so?
5. What is lightning?
6. Explain what causes thunder.
7. Which comes first – thunder or lightning?
8. How would you calculate the distance of a thunderstorm from you?
9. Many tall buildings use a lightning conductor that earths the electrical charge into the ground. Can you explain why?
10. Clouds, and thunder and lightning are natural wonders of the world. Make a list of others which appeal to you.

10 Rural life

In her very popular book *To School Through The Fields*, Alice Taylor tells the story of her childhood on a farm in Co. Cork. She wrote a poem about a little friend of hers whose hands had been badly burned. Can you picture the scene as the two of them made their way to school? 'We were reared as free as birds', writes Alice, 'growing up in a world of simplicity. We were free to be children, and to grow up at our own pace in a quiet place close to the earth.'

RURAL PEOPLE

Rural life has changed greatly since Alice Taylor made her way to school through the fields back in the 1940s. At that time about two-thirds of the people of the Republic of Ireland lived in the countryside. Then in the 1960s more and more people left the countryside to live in towns or cities. The distribution pattern changed so quickly that by 1971 more than half the people of the Republic (52 per cent) lived in towns. Nowadays only about one-third of our people live in the countryside.

URBAN PEOPLE

Urban dwellers depend very much on those who live in the countryside, because it is here that most of our food is produced. Just think of the food you will eat today, starting with the breakfast you had before you came to school. List out all the foods that come from a farm or were made from produce grown on the farm. Suppose we had no farmers! What do you think would happen then?

Along the western seaboard of Ireland there are many small farms. Some of these do not produce enough food even for the families who live on them. In other areas of the country such as the Golden Vale and the Plains of Meath, the yield from farms is very high. So, as well as supplying their own needs, these farmers are able to sell much of their agricultural produce.

RURAL LIFE

The pace of rural life is generally slower than that of urban life. There are few traffic jams, noise problems or housing shortages in the countryside. The air is clean and unpolluted. Compare the clear sparkling streams of the countryside with the dirty polluted rivers that flow through our cities. Rural people live close to the soil, which is a primary source of production. It is possible to live a natural, easy-going life there, away from the hustle and bustle of the city.

But of course there are disadvantages to rural living. Shops and schools can be a long distance away. When people become ill they may have to travel long distances to a hospital. Modern amenities such as the telephone, radio and television make country life so much easier now than it was in former times. And the countryside is not just for the people who live there – city people too can go there and enjoy its beauty. It is up to all of us to play our part in caring for the countryside.

THE COUNTRY CODE

Here are some rules that have been drawn up to guide us in the countryside. They are called the country code.

1. Do not damage fences, hedges and walls.
2. Respect the rights of landowners.
3. Close the gates if you open them.
4. Have consideration for others.
5. Respect the things of nature.
6. Take care on country roads.
7. Leave no litter.
8. Watch your dog.
9. Be careful with fire.
10. Keep to the paths.

TO DO

Learn the country code and sketch or paint some scenes to go with the different parts of the code.

A SCHOOL FRIEND

We walked to school
Through the dew drenched fields
Meeting where our paths crossed
At the foot of a grassy hill.
If one ran late, the other
Left a stone message
On the mossy bridge.
He had muddy boots,
A jumper torn by briars
And hair that went its own way.
Trivial details to a mind
That raced amongst the clouds
And followed rabbits down brown burrows.
Gentle hands, twisted by a bad burning,
Reached out towards the birds,
And they perched on his fingers
At ease with one of their own.
Blessed with a mind that ran free
From the frailties of his body
He walked during his quiet life
Close to the gates of heaven.
Alice Taylor

11 Let's play Dublin

What a splendid idea! In fact, we could even say it's a capital idea. Rather than sitting you down to a very ordinary lesson about Dublin, we want to take you out and about to discover some interesting information about our capital city.

THE POPULATION OF DUBLIN

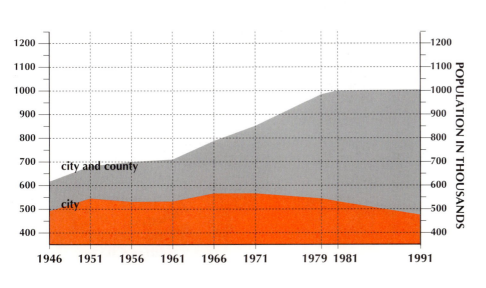

The people of Dublin celebrated the city's millenium in 1988. There is evidence to suggest that there was a settlement where Dublin is located well before 988 AD. If we look at a graph showing the growth of population in Dublin during the period after the Second World War we can see some really unusual trends.

QUESTIONS

1. What is a millenium? Do you know of any other Irish cities which have celebrated special anniversaries?
2. In 1946, 506,051 people lived in Dublin's County Borough. The County Borough is the Corporation area. It is also commonly called the City of Dublin. Approximately what percentage of Dublin's total population (636,193 people) lived in the city in 1946? You can use a calculator to work out the percentage if you wish.
3. In 1966 the corresponding figures were 568,772 (city) and 795,047 (city and county together). What percentage of the population now lived in the city? Try to explain the changes which have taken place since 1946.
4. Calculate the percentage living in Dublin City in 1991. The figures are 477,675 (city) and 1,024,429 (city and county together).
5. Try to explain why the population of Dublin County has increased so greatly between 1946 and 1991.

THE ZONES OF DUBLIN CITY

If we drove from the outskirts of Dublin into the very heart of the city, we would notice that the buildings in different places are used for a variety of purposes.

Community, social and leisure centre in Artane, Dublin

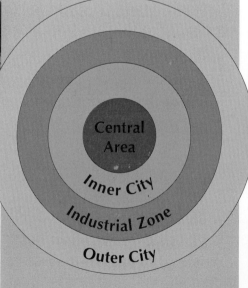

Central Area
Inner City
Industrial Zone
Outer City

52

THE OUTER CITY

We would first meet the outer city or the suburbs. In the suburbs we would mainly find family houses or flats. We would also see shopping centres in which people buy many of their day-to-day needs. Schools, churches, recreational buildings and open spaces are also found in this zone.

INDUSTRIAL ZONE

Many of Dublin's industrial estates are in the next zone. People can travel from their homes in the suburbs to work and back again. Because of this the suburbs are sometimes call dormitory areas. (A dormitory is where people sleep.)

THE INNER CITY

Over the past thirty years many people left their homes in Dublin's inner city for new homes in the suburbs. As in other large cities, there are parts of Dublin's inner city which are very run-down and shabby.

In the inner city areas we also find many large department stores, banks, cinemas and other services which people need.

URBAN RENEWAL

The inner parts of cities are usually the oldest. Because of this they often fall into disrepair. It is necessary to offer special low taxation rates to help redevelop the inner city.

The Irish Government announced a major plan called the Urban Renewal Act in 1985. The main aims of this act were to improve and bring life back to the inner parts of Dublin and other large Irish cities.

QUESTIONS

1. Can you explain why people buy most of their day-to-day needs in shopping centres near their homes?
2. People tend to buy items like furniture in the central areas of cities. Why is this?
3. Explain why land in the inner city can often be very expensive.
4. How can governments encourage people to move back into the inner city?
5. Why are services such as cinemas and insurance companies often located in the centre of a city?

Part of Dublin's Financial Services Centre

Dubliners

Can you name these famous Dublin people?

1. He was the writer of *Gulliver's Travels* and Dean of St. Patrick's Cathedral.
2. She is a comedienne and singer, Queen of the Dublin pantomimes.
3. He is a boxer from Crumlin who won a gold medal in Barcelona in 1992.
4. She is the first lady to become leader of an Irish political party.
5. He is a cyclist from Dundrum who won the world championships, the Tour de France and the Giro Italia all in one year.

Where in Dublin ...

1. ... are All-Ireland hurling, football and camogie finals played?
2. ... are rugby internationals played?
3. ... are the RTE television studios?
4. ... does the Dáil meet?
5. ... is the General Post Office?

LET'S PLAY DUBLIN

Our artist has designed a board game for part of Dublin's central area. Begin at the *start* square and use a dice to control your journey through the city. The first person to reach the *end* square is the winner.

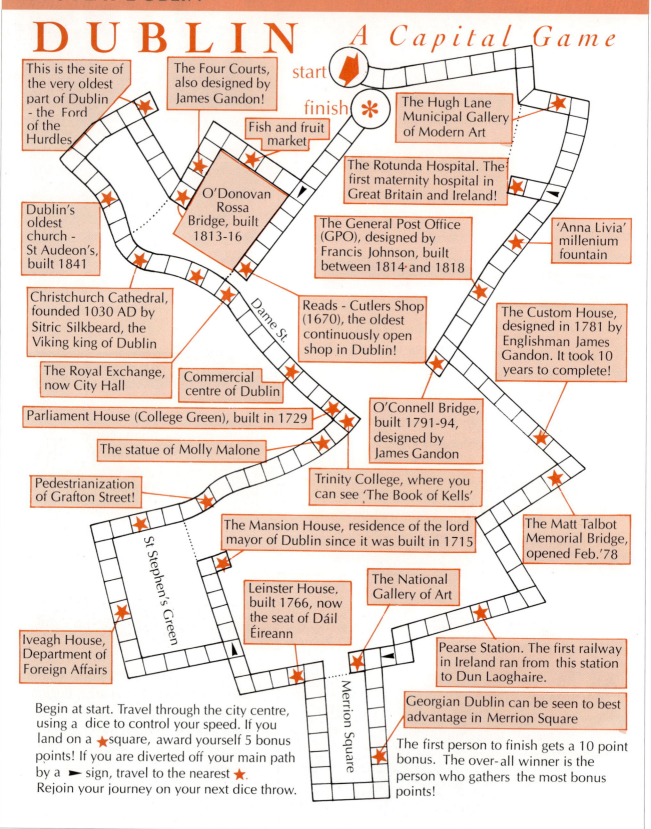

12 Climate and climatic change

Straight to work! In our *Worldwise* series we have looked at weather and climate in different parts of the world. Here is a map showing the major environmental regions of planet earth. Study it for a few minutes and then answer some questions.

MAJOR ENVIRONMENTAL REGIONS OF PLANET EARTH

- Ice-cap and tundra
- Mountain climates
- Desert climates
- Warm climates
- Cold climates
- Tropical climates

QUESTIONS

1. Where are the cold climates of the world?
2. Where are the tropical climates?
3. Can you name the major mountain ranges which have their own special environments?
4. Which continents in the following list have the greatest number of climatic environments?
   North America, South America, Africa, Australia and Eurasia.
5. Explain the difference between weather and climate.

57

CLIMATIC CHANGE

We know that the earth's climate has changed on several occasions in its history. Sometimes the temperature rose and at other times it actually dropped. The drops in temperature caused the great ice ages which we looked at in *Worldwise 3*. Now, once again the earth's climate seems to be changing. But this change is not a natural one – it is caused by people. We want to look at just one aspect of climatic change which is happening in our atmosphere. This is called the greenhouse effect.

THE GREENHOUSE EFFECT

The thin layer of air above us, called the atmosphere, is vital for life. Sadly, we continue to poison our air. Nature has designed a perfect balance for life to develop on earth. Yet we human beings think we know better.

We pollute the air in a number of ways. Our 'chimney chart' shows you the main sources of pollutants. Motor vehicles are by far the worst polluters, pumping millions of tonnes of carbon dioxide and nitrogen oxides into the air every year. Methane gas, belched from the front (and back!) end of cattle, from the rotting garbage of rubbish dumps, and from rice in paddy fields, adds to the pollution.

- 4% Other sources
- 6% Domestic sources
- 14% Power plants
- 16% Industry
- 60% Motor vehicles

These pollutants cannot escape into space. They are trapped in our atmosphere. They then act as a barrier to the heat trying to escape back out into space from the earth. So the pollution barrier, just like the glass roof of a greenhouse, prevents heat from escaping back into the atmosphere and the temperature of our atmosphere rises. Scientists suggest that within fifty years the temperature could be 2 or 3°C higher.

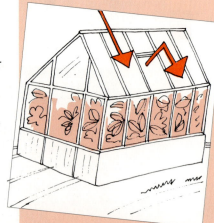

The glass on the roof reflects rising heat back in again.

58

That may not seem very much, but it would melt a lot of the ice at the north and south poles. Rising sea levels could devastate low-lying countries such as Bangladesh. And do you know something which is even sadder? The best single way that nature has for reducing carbon dioxide in the atmosphere is a forest of trees like we studied in Amazonia. Yet we destroy them at a rate of around 10 sq km every hour of every day in the year. The very smoke from the tree-burning itself adds to the polluted atmosphere and the greenhouse effect.

Rebuilding a home in Bangladesh after a cyclone

QUESTIONS

1. What is the greenhouse effect?
2. Why, do you think, have scientists given it this name?
3. Can you explain what causes it?
4. Name the worst single source of atmospheric pollution.
5. What suggestion have scientists made about the increase in the earth's temperature within the next fifty years?
6. What countries will be badly affected if the predicted rise in sea levels come true?
7. Will any parts of Ireland be affected by flooding?
8. Some scientists have complained that planet earth must be the biggest rubbish dump in the universe. Try to explain this comment.
9. Why is it so sad that we pollute our atmosphere and continue to destroy our forests?

Five steps in the right direction

Countries should begin to try to solve the greenhouse effect by

- imposing special taxes on vehicles which emit carbon dioxide.
- increasing research on alternative energy sources such as solar power.
- providing financial aid for developing nations to build energy-efficient power plants.
- planting vast numbers of trees.
- trapping at least part of the methane gas given off by rubbish tips and by cattle at feeding points.

13 Water and life

> **Water** – colourless, odourless, transparent fluid. May exist in three states – liquid, solid, gaseous.

This dictionary entry helps us look at a fluid which we call water. Water is far more than any of these definitions. It is the very basis of life itself.

Clonmacnoise on the River Shannon. Settlements grew where water flowed.

Life depends on a water supply.

WATER AND LIFE

We learned in *Worldwise 2* how primitive life began in water. Water accounts for between 50 per cent and 90 per cent of the weight of plants and animals. Our own bodies are composed of some two-thirds water.

The great rivers of the world always attracted people to settle close to them. The River Nile was famous in Egyptian legend for supplying water for drinking and irrigation. It even transported vast amounts of alluvium and deposited it in the Nile plains, where it made the most wonderfully fertile soils. Many of the world's great cities started as small settlements on river banks. Indeed, most of Ireland's cities developed in this way.

WATER DEMAND, SUPPLY AND TREATMENT

As the populations of countries have grown and as they have become more industrialised, the demands for water have become very much greater.

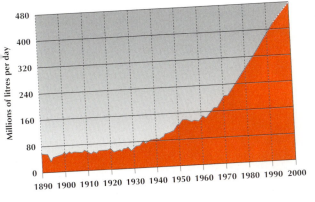

This line graph shows the average daily consumption of water in the Greater Dublin Area for the last 100 years. It also projects (predicts) demand up to the year 2000. The increase in demand is staggering, especially over the past 30 years.

Most of the water which we use in Ireland is taken from rivers and lakes. Engineers have designed huge reservoirs which store water for times of shortage and drought. Apart from storing water, reservoirs have another great advantage – they can help reduce the risk of flooding in times of very heavy rainfall.

The water supplied by Corporations and County Councils for domestic use must first be treated and purified. Every effort is made to ensure that the water we drink is fit for human consumption.

QUESTIONS

1. Name five domestic uses of water.
2. Why is domestic water quality more important than other uses, for example, general industrial uses?
3. Explain the term dehydration. How might dehydration happen?
4. Can you suggest why Dublin's water demands have increased so greatly over the past three decades?
5. What is the present daily consumption for the Dublin region?
6. Where might we find water in liquid, solid and gaseous forms?
7. What are the freezing and boiling points of water? Please give your answer in °C. This is a 100 mark question!
8. Why did great rivers like the Nile attract early settlers?
9. Name any five major Irish rivers and the cities which are built on their banks.
10. Name any five important world rivers and their cities.

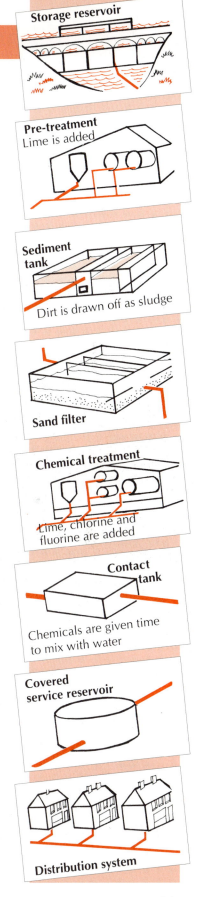

WATER IN THE DEVELOPING WORLD

People like ourselves are generally fortunate in being able to drink clean water. Not everybody in the world can do so. Up to 25 million people die of water-borne diseases every year. Sadly, over half of those who die are children like yourselves. Nearly all of these deaths take place in the poorer countries of the world which we call The Developing World. Poor sanitation is a major problem and open sewers often run side-by-side with waterways used for drinking water. Cholera and malaria are just two of the major killers which lurk in the waters of many developing countries.

TOO LITTLE WATER

We have often said in times of heavy flooding, 'Oh, how I wish it would stop raining.' Spare a thought for those who suffer quite a different problem – water shortage.

If we asked you to explain the word 'desert', what would you say? The words 'hot', 'dry', 'sandy' and 'deserted' come to mind perhaps. All of these descriptions are partly true. Hot deserts get less than 250mm of rain every year. All of this rain may fall in just a single heavy downpour. The day-time temperatures are very hot and at times reach 50°C. While these areas are very hot during the day, they are freezing at night-time because the clear, cloudless skies allow all of the heat to escape back into the atmosphere.

PEOPLE AND DESERTS

They are not the most attractive places to live in, yet over 500 million people spend their lives in the world's deserts. Desert people live their lives either at the settlements built near oases or as nomads wandering through the desert from oasis to oasis. Among the best known of these are the Bedouin tribes.

Attempts have been made to reclaim desert lands for agriculture, but this is a very expensive process. As we try to reclaim some land, deserts are growing around the world because people mismanage their environment.

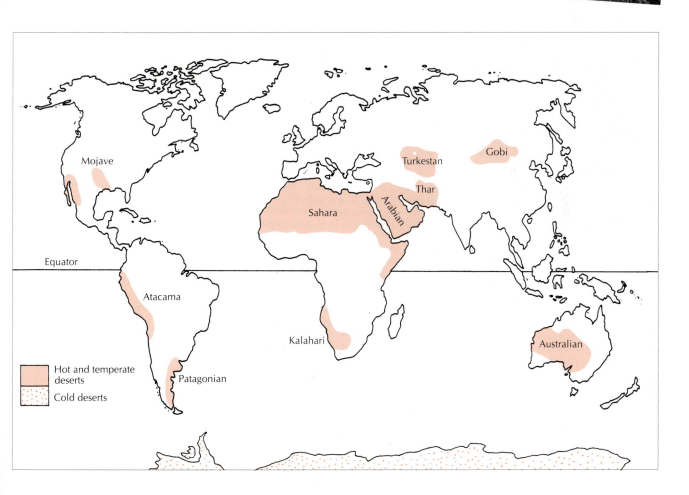

Some Special Soils

Soil particles can also be blown by strong winds. You will have noticed this if you live by a coast and have seen sand being blown by the wind. Vast amounts of soil are transported by wind in China. These soils are called *loess*.

Rivers can also transport particles of soil for many kilometres. Soils which have been transported and deposited by rivers are called alluvial soils.

A child of the desert

An oasis in the desert

QUESTIONS

1. Nearly all of the world's hot deserts are located between 15° and 30° north and south of the equator. Name five of these deserts. Where are the world's cold deserts? Hint – north and south!
2. Write down some words or phrases which describe hot deserts.
3. Why might people choose to live in a desert?
4. Explain why deserts are such difficult environments for people to live in.
5. You have been stranded in a desert landscape. Describe your survival efforts before you are finally rescued by some nomadic people. In your description consider the problems of water and food shortages, the likely effects on your health and the possibility of mirages.

14 The explosive earth

We tend to think of the earth beneath our feet as being rock solid. Sometimes when we get a little too big for our shoes, our parents chide us with the line – 'Hang on! Keep your feet on the ground.'

In many parts of the world the ground moves and does so very violently. We will explain why in this chapter.

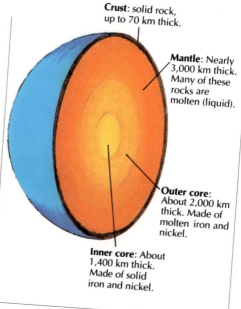

Crust: solid rock, up to 70 km thick.

Mantle: Nearly 3,000 km thick. Many of these rocks are molten (liquid).

Outer core: About 2,000 km thick. Made of molten iron and nickel.

Inner core: About 1,400 km thick. Made of solid iron and nickel.

PLANET EARTH

The planet we live on was formed around 4,600 million years ago. It began its life as a fiery mass. The crust of the earth cooled down, over many millions of years, but the inside is still made of hot (molten) liquid rock. People have often said that the earth is like a bowl of porridge which has cooled down – a crusted layer forms on top but the inside still flows quite easily.

A volcano erupting in Hawaii, USA

PLATES

The earth's crust floats on top of the hot liquid rock. This crust is made of a series of slabs which we call plates. The plates fit together like a huge jigsaw. Some of the plates are moving apart while other are slowly crashing into each other.

As hard as flint

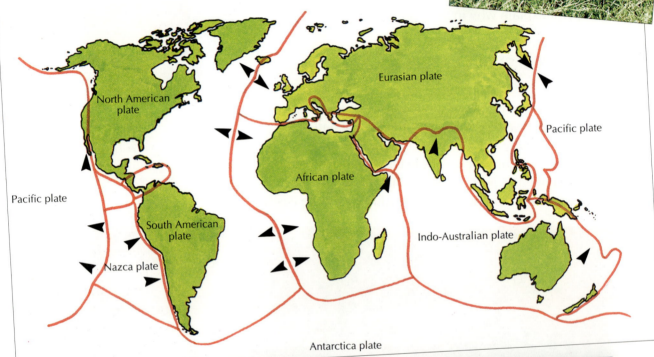

QUESTIONS

Study this map showing the earth's plates and answer some questions.
1. Scientists tell us the earth is about _____ years old.
2. Where would you find the earth's core?
3. What do we call the outer, solid layer of the earth?
4. What is the inner part of the earth made of?
5. How are the earth's plates moving?
6. On what plate is Ireland located?
7. North America and Europe are moving apart by about 2cm every year. Where is this movement taking place? Hint – out in the water!
8. Name the plate south of the Mediterranean Sea.
9. Where is the Nazca Plate?
10. What does the old saying 'keep your feet on the ground' mean?

DANCE OF THE CONTINENTS

A huge super-continent called *Pangea* broke up into separate continents about 250 million years ago. Over millions of years the continents drifted into their present positions.

Pangea – the huge super-continent – was appropriately named. The word means 'all earth'.

We know the continents on the plates are still moving. Nearly every year, the earth itself tells us so. It announces this by violent displays of force which we know as volcanoes and earthquakes.

Kilavea volcano, Hawaii

VOLCANOES

The edges of the earth's plates are called margins. These are dangerous places in which to live because it is on these that most of the 1,000 active volcanoes on earth are located. Perhaps the best way to understand a volcanic eruption is to consider what happens when you shake a bottle of fizzy drink and then suddenly open the cap. What happens? The drink erupts! The same build-up of pressure takes place within a volcano, and when it becomes very great, the lava and ash are released as a volcanic eruption.

EARTHQUAKES

Earthquakes are even more frightening than volcanic eruptions. The earth's plates are constantly moving. Before an earthquake takes place the plates are stuck together. Suddenly the plates may slip and then huge shock waves spread out. The point where the two plates are moving against each other, sending out the tremors, is called the epicentre. This is where the greatest destruction takes place. Scientists measure the strength of an earthquake with an instrument called a seismograph, on a scale called the Richter scale.

Cracks in the earth caused by earthquake, California

QUESTIONS

1. Explain how a volcano erupts.
2. Volcanic eruptions are usually more spectacular than dangerous. Why?
3. Earthquakes are very dangerous acts of nature. Why is this?
4. Explain how an earthquake is caused.
5. What do we call the point at which the greatest pressure is released during an earthquake?

TO DO

Find out a little more about famous volcanic eruptions and earthquakes in history. Your research can include recent happenings as well as historical events like Vesuvius and Krakatoa.

You can have some really interesting fun putting the continents together again. Cut out the shapes of the continents and try to fit them together like a jig-saw. Use the map of Pangea as a guide to how our continents were once joined.

15 Maps and skills

The oldest map in the world was drawn on a tablet of soft clay. It was done over 4,000 years ago by a tax-collector who lived in ancient Babylonia. He needed to know how much land every person owned so that he could collect tax from them. Instead of writing it out in a long list, he drew a map of the area instead.

Ever since, people have used maps to store information about their environments. Today, most maps are printed on paper but in earlier times they were printed on many different materials, even timber. In fact the latin word *mappa* means a napkin, indicating that in early Roman times maps were printed on cloth.

OUR WORLD THIS WEEK

WORLD MAPS

So many events and disasters happen around the world every day that we often find it difficult to store all of the place images in our minds. Some newspapers provide little maps when reporting a story from foreign countries, but to follow events properly we really need to use either a large wall-map or an atlas.

South Africa ....

Germany ....

USA ....

Australia ....

Northern Ireland ....

Japan ....

Here is an interesting and useful exercise for you. Make out a list of the world's most 'evident' countries every week. An evident country is one that is in the news. You can use newspapers, television news, radio news or a good national/international news magazine to help you follow events. Make a list of perhaps 10 or 12 countries towards the end of your school-week and as a home exercise find these places in your atlas. For your next Geography lesson try to know the countries well enough to be able to mark them on a large blank map of the world.

IRISH MAPS

We are very fortunate to have such a long and excellent tradition of map-making in Ireland. We still have very many rather old historical maps showing all or parts of Ireland from the time of the Great Plantations onwards. We can usually get photocopies of these made by a local or county library. Try to get such a map for your own local area and see how the place has changed since the map was made. Compare this map with a modern Ordnance Survey map for your locality. What scale is used on these maps?

An aerial photograph can give us a clear picture of a large area of the countryside. Satellite pictures show even larger areas. By 1969 only a quarter of the country of Peru had been mapped. Then a satellite flew over and in three minutes it provided photographs of the entire country.

THE ORDNANCE SURVEY

The official mapping of Ireland is carried out by the Ordnance Survey. Its headquarters is in the Phoenix Park in Dublin. It has been located in the very same buildings since it was first set up in Ireland in 1824. Because it has such a long tradition of excellent service, it is a wonderful source of information about our historical and present-day landscapes. A lot of work has to be carried out to make a map.

Today, the Ordnance Survey uses the most up-to-date technology, including computers and aerial reconnaissance, to make modern maps of Ireland.

Uses of Maps

Map skills are life skills. We use maps so frequently that we can appreciate just how true the old saying is. Here is the old saying, in code! Can you figure it out?

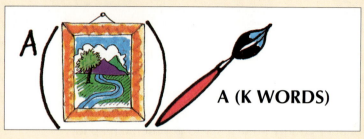

A (K WORDS)

Turn the page upside down if you want to break the code.

A picture paints a thousand words.

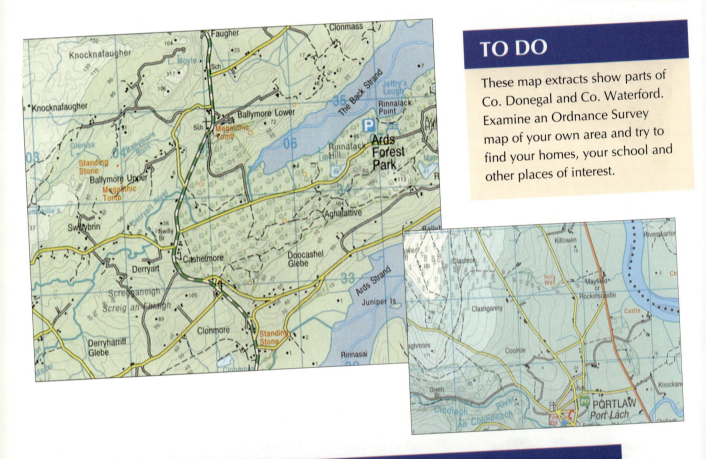

TO DO

These map extracts show parts of Co. Donegal and Co. Waterford. Examine an Ordnance Survey map of your own area and try to find your homes, your school and other places of interest.

TO DO

In *Worldwise 2* we used a simple distance chart for the first time. The distance chart on page 73 covers 46 Irish towns and gives the number of kilometres between any two towns.

You can use two rulers if you wish to work in pairs on this exercise. Work out the distances between any 10 pairs of towns you care to choose on the map. It's a very useful exercise and helps us to plan our journeys in a sensible and efficient way.

KILOMETRE CHART

Athlone																				
137	Ballina																			
219	269	Belfast																		
113	249	251	Carlow																	
140	273	330	90	Clonmel																
219	296	421	187	97	Cork															
232	198	119	296	362	436	Derry														
180	122	187	285	320	394	76	Donegal													
127	247	166	82	164	256	237	227	Dublin												
142	330	82	167	248	340	159	164	84	Dundalk											
111	173	330	185	116	136	333	270	237	253	Ennis										
90	119	301	188	185	206	278	203	217	233	68	Galway									
116	252	280	39	50	146	323	296	114	198	148	172	Kilkenny								
226	309	446	235	146	85	459	407	304	368	146	206	196	Killarney							
117	200	336	138	79	101	349	297	204	251	37	105	111	109	Limerick						
179	261	402	167	79	35	410	358	237	320	98	158	129	68	66	Mallow					
47	164	177	100	161	235	209	174	87	95	158	137	117	262	150	215	Mullingar				
71	208	245	37	100	174	277	243	84	155	151	143	48	224	113	154	68	Portlaoise			
115	58	209	182	256	330	140	65	217	169	206	138	231	343	233	295	137	187	Sligo		
140	246	348	114	39	85	360	312	179	259	76	143	75	134	39	66	153	95	248	Tipperary	
220	305	442	253	172	117	455	400	306	348	143	203	212	32	101	82	256	214	340	134	Tralee
164	301	328	76	48	124	372	336	163	246	164	233	48	195	127	127	161	97	280	87	209	Waterford
183	320	301	77	109	185	372	362	135	203	225	253	81	256	188	188	180	113	299	148	288	61	Wexford
170	296	214	87	179	251	285	275	51	132	277	261	129	325	239	257	142	114	265	201	341	142	87	Wicklow

16 Children of the world

'Today's children are tomorrow's world.' This is a simple statement but it is also very true. In this chapter we are going to look at our world through the eyes and lives of children and remind ourselves of some of the rights and responsibilities which we all have as people.

HUMAN RIGHTS

The United Nations (UN) is truly a world organisation. Its headquarters is in New York and it has a membership of 184 countries. The principal aim of the United Nations is to preserve international peace and security.

Wars and conflicts often arise within countries and between countries. The United Nations is quite aware that these conflicts have a variety of causes. Some conflicts occur between powerful and powerless groups of people. Others may be based on political, social, cultural, economic, racial or religious disputes. Whatever the causes, and whether or not the causes are just or unjust, we can be sure about some basic facts. Conflicts are far easier to start than to finish. Discussion, not force, is the way to resolve conflict.

Three years after its foundation in 1945, the United Nations agreed on a Universal Declaration of Human Rights. Here are some of the most important human rights. Look closely at them and then answer the questions.

Human Rights

Everybody should have the right to:
- Life, freedom and personal security
- Food, clothing, shelter and a reasonable standard of living
- Work and rest
- Health and education
- Freedom of thought and enjoyment of their own religious beliefs and conscience
- Meetings and peaceful assembly
- Their own nationality
- Ownership of their own property
- A life free of torture, slavery or ill-treatment
- A world order (system) which guarantees all of these rights.

QUESTIONS

1. Why are today's children tomorrow's world?
2. Name any three important rights you have as a person.
3. What do we mean when we say that we have responsibilities as people? Give some examples.
4. Can you suggest why the United Nations was founded in 1945? Hint – War and Peace.
5. Are you aware of any wars or conflicts in the world today? Give some examples.
6. Why are these conflicts taking place?
7. Explain these statements: Conflicts are far easier to start than to finish. Discussion, not force, is the solution to conflict.
8. Irish peace-keeping forces have served the United Nations in several countries. Find these places in your atlas: Iran-Iraq Border, Cyprus, India-Pakistan Border, Namibia, Lebanon, Afghanistan-Pakistan Border, Congo, Israel, Syria.
9. Why, do you think, did the United Nations feel it necessary to proclaim a Universal Declaration of Human Rights?
10. Put the ten human rights into the order which you think is important. We call this a ranking exercise. Go from 1 (most important) to 10 (least important). Discuss your ranking in class.

CHILDREN AND RIGHTS

Children do not have political power. They depend totally on their parents or guardians to protect their rights. Sadly, these rights are not protected for many children in the world today. A number of children are abused and also at times exploited by those parents who are supposed to protect them. An even greater number of children are denied their rights by forces outside the control of their families. Wars and natural disasters, unemployment, poverty and a lack of education can all conspire against children.

Some governments still use children to fight their wars. Some employers still exploit children by paying them wages that are totally unjust. Some countries seem unaware that we all share a common humanity and that resources must be shared in a just way.

In 1989, on the tenth anniversary of the International Year of the Child, the General Assembly of the United Nations adopted an International Convention on the Rights of the Child. The convention (agreement) recognised that children needed help to survive, to be protected and to be allowed develop as full people. It is the responsibility of every person and every government to make sure that these rights are protected.

TO DO

In the world today one person in every eight does not have enough to eat. How would you solve the problem of world hunger? Discuss the following reasons which are often used to explain world hunger and famines. A word of warning – not all of them are true and we indicate those that are correct by this sign ✓.

People are hungry because
- There is not enough food in the world.
- There are too many people in the world and families in poor countries often have too many children.
- Droughts and other natural disasters make food production very difficult in some countries. ✓
- Modern farming methods can be found only in developed countries.
- Developed countries use far more pesticides, insecticides and fertilisers to produce much larger quantities of food. ✓
- Poorer countries cannot afford to buy enough food. ✓
- Many developing countries have governments which do not help their people to get enough food. ✓
- Large tracts of land in developing countries are owned by rich landowners and foreign companies. ✓
- Developing countries owe large amounts of money (foreign debts) to international banks. ✓
- There is no solution to the problem of hunger which has existed throughout history.
- The richer countries of the world do not share the world's resources with the poorer countries. ✓
- The world's trade system favours the larger richer countries. ✓

Do you know?

A person needs a supply of about 2,500 calories every day to maintain a proper quality of life. Let us call this figure 100 per cent of daily requirements. Find the following countries in your atlas and consider their average daily supplies of calories. Those above 100 per cent have too much food while those below have too little food.

	PER CENT
Bangladesh	78
France	142
Ghana	78
Greece	145
Haiti	79
Ireland	140
Italy	143
Mali	69
Mozambique	68
USA	140

17 Effortless power – with the flick of a switch

Strong winds may bring about major changes in our lives. If they bring down electricity cables, our homes may be without power for several hours. When a power loss takes place on a cold winter evening we very quickly see how dependent we are on electricity. Candles or torches replace electric light bulbs, and heating and cooking systems may also be out of action.

HISTORY OF ELECTRICITY

There are many forms of electrical energy in our natural world. In chapter 9 we looked at the formation of lightning. Benjamin Franklin, an American scientist, flew kites into thunderstorms in 1753, to conduct an electrical charge along the flying cord. He did invent a lightning conductor but was also very fortunate to have survived such a crazy act. He could easily have been killed.

Michael Faraday, an English scientist, invented the dynamo in 1831 and made the first big break-through by using magnetism to make electricity. Another famous invention was that of the light-bulb. This is credited to Thomas Edison of America in 1878.

CYCLE POWER

If you have ever cycled a bicycle after dusk, you have probably used a dynamo to produce your own power. Our first type of dynamo is in the middle of the front wheel. When the wheel turns, an electric current is made inside the dynamo. This electricity lights up the front and rear lamps when the switch is turned on.

At the centre of the dynamo there is a coil of wire, fixed in position. Outside that there is a round-shaped magnet. The magnet turns around the coil when the wheel moves. This turning of the magnet around the coil creates a flow of electricity in the coil. The electric current flows from the coil to light up the bulbs in the lamps.

Another type of dynamo looks like a bottle and it is fixed to the wheel. We can see, from our artwork, how it works. As before, the magnet rotates and the coil of wire remains fixed in position. The electric current which is made in the coil is used to light up the lamps.

Another name for a dynamo is a generator – it generates electric current from movement. In the case of the cycle dynamo the movement is provided by the pedalling of the cyclist. Pedalling can be hard work and burns up lots of energy. We can show that chain of events in a flow-chart.

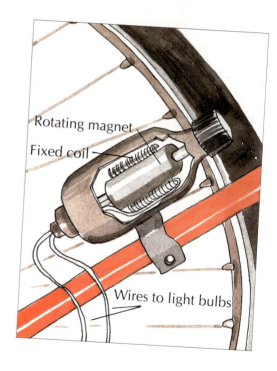

GLUCOSE ➤ ENERGY ➤ MOVEMENT ➤ ELECTRICITY ➤ LIGHT

MAKING ELECTRICITY

The electricity we use in our homes is made in the same way as that in the cycle dynamo. A stronger flow of electricity can be produced by using bigger magnets, faster movement and more loops of wire in the coil.

The Five Lamps, Dublin

QUESTIONS

1. Name some of the ways which show that we depend a lot on electricity.
2. What did Benjamin Franklin discover in 1753?
3. What discovery did Michael Faraday make?
4. How does a bicycle dynamo produce power?
5. Since energy is burned up very rapidly by hard cycling we want you to suggest some foods that could be eaten by top international athletes like Sonia O'Sullivan. Remember, these foods must be high in energy and able to release it quickly into the body.

THE ESB

In 1892 the Corporation of Dublin provided electricity to parts of Dublin through their Electric Lighting Committee. It was 35 years later, however, before an organisation was formed which would supply electricity to all of Ireland. This organisation is called the Electricity Supply Board (ESB).

The ESB has several generating stations throughout the country. The purpose of these stations is to convert movement into electric current. The ESB provides movement in two different ways – by falling water and by the force of steam.

ELECTRICITY FROM FALLING WATER

Electricity stations that use falling water to generate current are called hydro-electric stations. *Hydro* is a Greek word meaning water. When water falls from a height it can easily be used to turn the blades of a turbine.

Ardnacrusha hydro-electric scheme

As the turbine rotates, so too does a magnet fixed overhead. The magnet, which is itself large, is surrounded by a huge coil of wire and just as in the case of the cycle dynamo, the movement of the magnet creates a flow of electricity in the coil.

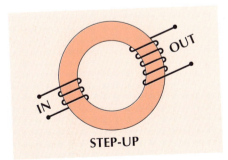
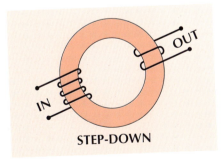

The electric current is fed into a transformer which increases its strength even more. This diagram shows how the strength of the current can be made three time stronger by having three times as many loops of output wire as there are of input wire.

81

Electricity Power Stations

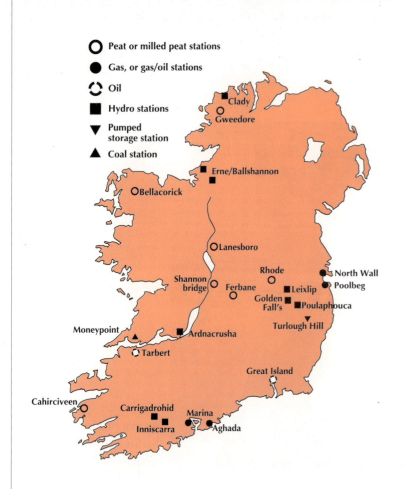

Poolbeg power station

QUESTIONS

Look at the map of electricity generating stations and answer the following questions.

1. How many hydro-electric stations are operated by the ESB?
2. Name something that they all have in common.
3. Name the three stations on the River Liffey.
4. Why do you think this river was chosen by the ESB?
5. Name the two stations on the River Lee.
6. What large city is near these stations?
7. What river is harnessed at Ardnacrusha?
8. On what river is the Ballyshannon generating station?
9. What kind of countryside is most suitable for hydro-electric stations?
10. Name other countries that have this kind of countryside.

TURLOUGH HILL

The ESB generating station at Turlough Hill, Co. Wicklow is a very interesting use of natural resources. It is an example of a pumped-storage station. A huge reservoir or lake has been made on top of the hill. Water is pumped up to the reservoir from Lough Nahangan, 270 metres below. This is done at periods of the day when there is not a great demand for electricity. At these times the level of water in the reservoir is raised.

When demand for power is great, the water is released back down through the tunnel which has been built through the heart of the hill. It eventually goes back into the lake below. On its way down the falling water hits and turns the blades of a turbine in just the same way as we saw with the hydro-electric stations.

The huge reservoir at Turlough Hill

ELECTRICITY FROM STEAM

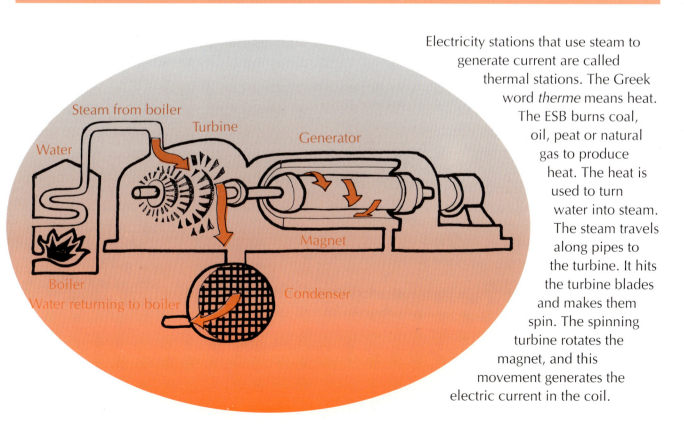

Electricity stations that use steam to generate current are called thermal stations. The Greek word *therme* means heat. The ESB burns coal, oil, peat or natural gas to produce heat. The heat is used to turn water into steam. The steam travels along pipes to the turbine. It hits the turbine blades and makes them spin. The spinning turbine rotates the magnet, and this movement generates the electric current in the coil.

83

DEMAND FOR ELECTRICITY

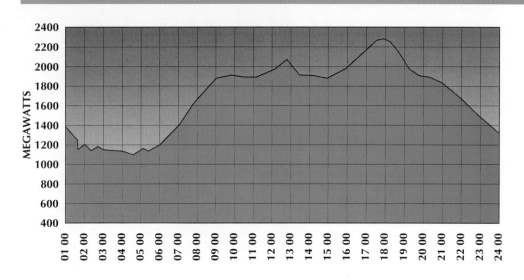

We can use a graph to show the use of electricity throughout the day. On it we can see the periods when we need least and most electricity.

This graph shows that the use of electricity is not even throughout the day and night.

QUESTIONS

1. How many ESB stations use peat to provide the necessary heat?
2. In what kind of countryside do you think these stations are situated?
3. What company harvests the peat for sale to the ESB?
4. Which stations use natural gas? Where does this fuel come from?
5. Name the stations that use imported oil. Where, do you think, might this oil come from?
6. Electricity in Northern Ireland is produced by the NIEB. What do these letters stand for?
7. At what time of the day is the demand for electricity greatest? Give reasons for this.
8. When does the least demand for electricity occur? Why is this?
9. How would you explain the rise in demand for electricity just after mid-day?
10. The rural electrification scheme changed the Irish landscape. How do you think it did this?

TO DO

Electricity is one of the most powerful and dangerous forms of energy. It can kill instantly. Design and colour a safety poster in class. If you want more information on electricity, one person from your class can write to the ESB Public Relations Department at their Dublin Headquarters. You will find the address in a telephone directory.

18 Little and large ... countries of the world

Isn't it fascinating? When we look down from space we see a world without borders. We see a world without war – a world very much at peace with itself. Yet when we come down to earth it is very easy to see a world divided. We can look at this division at different scales (levels).

NORTH AND SOUTH

It is very common to look at the world as groups of countries which make up units called 'blocs'. There is a First World Bloc – made up of industrialised countries which are very developed economically. Ireland is a First World country. The Second World is made of countries whose economies are centrally planned – these are communist countries. China is a Second World country. The final bloc is the Third World. This consists of well over 100 countries which are far less developed than the First and Second World. Most of the less-developed countries are located in the southern hemisphere.

A hard-worked child of the Third World

UNEQUAL SHARES

The world has a long history of exploitation. This means that stronger countries (or people) have used their power to conquer weaker countries and take their lands and resources for themselves. Many natural resources such as oil or metals have been robbed from the weaker countries with the result that today some developing countries are very poor. They depend for their trade on the richer First World countries. But sadly the terms of trade are very much stacked against them. They have huge foreign debts and great difficulty in repaying loans and interest.

Northern Hemisphere

- 25% of the world's people
- 80% of the world's income
- People can expect to live up to 75 years on average
- Approximately 90% of the world's manufacturing industry
- Most people have enough to eat

Southern Hemisphere

- 75% of the world's people
- 20% of the world's income
- People can expect to live an average of 50 years
- Only 10% of the world's manufacturing industry
- One person in every five is hungry and malnourished

QUESTIONS

1. What are the three major 'blocs' of the world?
2. How do the 'blocs' differ from each other?
3. Why do people sometimes refer to the North-South divide in the world?
4. How has exploitation by developed countries affected less developed countries?
5. What percentage of the world's population lives in (a) the North and (b) the South?
6. What income differences can be found between the two hemispheres?
7. What is the life expectancy in (a) the Northern Hemisphere, (b) the Southern Hemisphere?
8. How would you account for the difference in the length of life people can expect to live?
9. The quality of life experienced by people in countries such as Ethiopia is quite different to that of most Irish people. Can you explain why this is so?

COUNTRIES OF THE WORLD

Some of the world's countries such as Monaco and the Vatican are quite tiny, while others such as China are very large indeed. Nearly all countries are organised as nation states. The majority of countries were created during the twentieth century. Most African states, for example, have been created since the end of the Second World War.

Nation States

- have clearly defined borders.
- share a common culture with common laws.
- have governments elected by their people.
- have governments which are usually located in capital cities.

PEACE AND WAR

The history of our world is littered with wars but we seem to have learned very little from our history. Countries still maintain huge armies and the threat of nuclear war will never disappear until we truly declare that the world is a place of peace.

Do remember that peace begins with people, not with countries. It begins with ordinary people like ourselves. Keep this chapter title in mind when next you see somebody small or weak being exploited and hurt.

TO DO

You can chose any or all of these three exercises. They will provide you with some new ways of looking at your world.

Neighbours

My apple trees will never get across and eat the cones under his pines, I tell him. He only says 'Good fences make good neighbours.'
Robert Frost (1914)

What message do these lines have for us?

War Games

In Star Wars T-shirts,
Armed with the Airfix bomber,
The young avengers
Crawl across the carpet
To blast the wastepaper basket
Into oblivion.

Later,
Curled on the sofa,
They watched unflinching
An edited version
Of War of the Day,
Only half-listening
As the newsreader
Lists the latest statistics.
Cushioned by distance,
How can they comprehend
The real score?

After *John Foster*

Election Time

Most nation states today have democratic ways of electing their governments. Democracy began in ancient Greece. It is a way of life in which every person is regarded as being as important and as valuable as the next. Everybody has the right to join in making decisions which affect their lives. One of the most important parts of democracy is the right to vote. Find out how the Irish voting system called Proportional Representation works. You can ask your teacher, your parents and perhaps your local TD, for advice on running a class election.

Discuss the way we allow children grow up with 'safe' images of war in comics, and 'real' images of war on television news.

19 Down to earth

Try to imagine a world without soil. We then have to imagine a world without food. We depend completely on the soils of planet earth for our survival.

ORIGIN OF SOILS

If we plant some seeds on a handful of rocks, are we likely to have any dramatic results? The answer of course is no – rocks cannot support extensive plant growth. And yet, these very rocks are the origin of the soil which is so vitally important to our life on earth. When natural processes of weathering break down rocks into small particles, we are looking at the start of soil formation.

Air and water go into the spaces between tiny rock particles and cause chemical changes to take place. Bacteria and simple plant life appear and when the plants die, they decay. Decaying plants and animals are broken down by bacteria into a black sticky material called humus. Humus is very important for soil fertility.

WHAT DO SOILS CONTAIN?

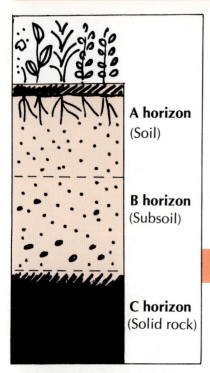

A horizon (Soil)
B horizon (Subsoil)
C horizon (Solid rock)

Soils are a mixture of different materials. First of all there is the humus which comes from the decayed plants. Then there are mineral particles which are produced from rocks by the weathering of wind and rain. Soils also contain water and air. Finally, soils contain tiny living organisms, especially bacteria.

SOIL PROFILES

If you have ever seen a road being widened or a quarry being opened, you may have noticed a soil profile. Soil profiles show us the different stages of soil development. The C horizon is made of rock and it is usually from this rock the soils develop. The B horizon generally contains a lot of stones and is not very fertile. The layer nearest the ground (A horizon) contains most humus and is the most fertile.

At times we need to examine a depth of soil in order to see horizons.

Soil

Humus

Mineral soil

Vegetation

Climate

Weathering

Parent rock

SOILS AND PEOPLE

People have cultivated soils for several thousand years and their main interest has usually been in soil fertility. Farmers use artificial fertilisers and natural manures from animals to keep soils fertile or to make them more fertile. Growing crops on different pieces of land over a number of years is called crop rotation and also helps soils to remain fertile.

More and more people are being attracted to growing and eating crops which are produced without artificial fertilisers. These foods are grown organically and their popularity is part of a 'green revolution' where people are becoming very aware of their natural environment.

All over Europe people are becoming more aware of the quality of organic foods. It is to be hoped that Irish food producers will benefit from this in the years ahead. Ireland has an excellent image abroad for having a pollution-free atmosphere.

TO DO

Bring in some soil samples for your next Geography lesson or try these experiments at home. Put some old newspapers on your work surface and they will keep it clean and tidy.

Experiment 1 – DESCRIBING

Take a soil sample and feel it with your fingers. How would you describe it? Is it rough or smooth? Is it wet or dry? What are its colours?

Look at the soil under a magnifying glass. Can you see any plant remains? Are there any tiny creatures or their remains in the soil?

Add some water to the soil. Squeeze it into a ball.
Does it remain as a ball, or does it fall apart? What might this tell us about the soil?

Experiment 2 – SORTING

You will need a sieve for this experiment. Begin by weighing a soil sample and recording its weight. Then remove the larger stones and put those in one pile. Do the same with the finer particles which go through a sieve. The third sub-sample will be left in the sieve. You can label the three samples as coarse, medium and fine soils. Weigh each sample and find out what percentage it forms of the full sample. What might this tell us about different soils?

Experiment 3 – DRAINING

Fill an empty yoghurt pot almost to the top with soil. Pack it firmly but don't press too hard on the soil. Punch a hole with a pencil into the bottom of the pot and then sit it onto a larger empty container. Use a pencil at the side of the container to create a natural air-space. Pour water from another pot into the yoghurt pot and measure the length of time it takes for all of the water to flow through the soil. If your friends use similar sized pots and containers you can compare results. How might soil drainage be important for farmers?

Experiment 4 – TESTING

Most large garden centres stock soil testing kits and they are not very expensive. A group of you from class could share the cost of one and then pass it from person to person, so everybody gets to use it. Use the kit to test the pH level of soil samples. The results will be in the range pH 6 and below (very acid) to pH 8 and above (very alkaline). Try to find the names of some plants which are 'lime-lovers' or 'lime-haters'. A good well-informed gardener will be able to help you. Why might it be important for gardeners to know their soil acidity?

20 A continent develops

Africa is a word. It may have come from the Latin word *Aprica* (sunny) or perhaps from the Greek word *Aphrike* (without cold).

Africa is a continent. In a traditional sense, the Red Sea acts as its boundary in the north-east. The Suez Canal – built in 1869 – completed the physical separation from Asia.

Africa is its people. Europeans have often spoken of Africa as the 'Dark Continent'. This was partly due to the skin colour of many of its people. It was also due to the lack of European knowledge and understanding about Africa.

Africa is its history. To understand present-day Africa, its people and problems, we also need to begin to understand its history.

THE HISTORY OF AFRICA

It is widely accepted that Eastern Africa is the cradle of 'modern' people. We use the word 'modern' against the span of the earth's history. While Ireland is thought to have been inhabited for around 9,000 years and Asia for at least 500,000 years, it is thought that our ancient ancestors evolved in Africa over several million years.

The great Egyptian culture, centred strongly on the River Nile, was Africa's first urban civilisation. Before the birth of Christ, the Greeks and Romans had conquered Egypt. Among the treasured items they brought out of Africa were ostrich feathers for decoration and wild animals to fight with gladiators. The Romans used to say, 'There is always something new from Africa.'

After the fall of the Roman Empire, Arabs swept across North Africa as far as Morocco. They brought with them their language, the religion of Islam, and Arabic culture. Northern Africa is thought of as part of the Arab world to this very day.

Throughout the rest of Africa, various kingdoms grew and declined. The kingdom of Ghana, the empire of Mali, and the empire of Gao governed West Africa between the fourth and fifteenth centuries AD. The native black cultures of East Africa were mixed with Arabic culture during the eighth century. Out of this mixture came the Swahili language and culture which survive in much of East Africa today.

EUROPEANS AND AFRICA

The Portuguese were the first Europeans to move south beyond the Sahara. Arab slave trade had existed for many years. The Portuguese turned the buying and selling of human beings into a full-scale industry. Other European countries such as The Netherlands, Great Britain and France quickly joined in.

It is widely agreed that between 15 and 20 million African people were sold into slavery in the Americas between 1500 and 1900 AD. It is also agreed that for every person sold, up to nine others died in the slave-hunt or on board the slave-ships. On this basis, nearly 200 million young, able-bodied African women and men were lost to their native continent.

COLONIAL CONQUEST

By the year 1875, one-tenth of Africa had been colonised by European countries. Ten years later, only one-tenth of Africa remained free.

COLONY
A colony is a settlement formed in a territory by people from another place. The new settlers (colonists) usually control the territory in which they settle.

The colonists used Africa to get raw materials for European industries. They also began a type of trade which still lasts today. Many crops such as cocoa were grown in Africa and exported to European countries. These crops are called cash crops since they are sold for cash.

This unfair system of trade, where less developed countries depend on just a few cash crops for much of their export earning, survives today. It has its roots, however, in colonial times. Cash crops take up valuable land which could be used for food crops. As a result, many African countries have to import large quantities of food to feed their people.

When Europeans gained their territories through conquest, they ignored important racial, religious, cultural and tribal boundaries. After African countries became independent – virtually all of them after World War 2 – their boundaries remained much as the colonists had drawn them. Many wars have since been fought within and between African countries.

THE FUTURE OF AFRICA

Africa's population growth rate of 3 per cent is the most rapid of all the continents. In 1993, its population was around 670 million people. If Africa's population continues to grow at its present rate it will double within twenty-five years.

African countries do need food aid in times of famine. They also really need financial aid, from the developed nations of the northern hemisphere. This should be used to help development. They need a fairer system of world trade which will guarantee markets and prices for the goods they wish to sell on world markets.

AFRICAN REFLECTIONS

Food Aid

'Food aid is the fertiliser of a rich crop called hunger'

Julius Nyerere
President of Tanzania

What did President Nyerere mean? How could food aid sent to developing countries from developed countries, help to continue the problem of hunger?

Nelson Mandela

Nelson Mandela spent nearly 28 years of his life in South African prisons for opposing the system of apartheid. This guaranteed that white-skinned people would have power over their black-skinned fellow country people. Find out more about apartheid and Nelson Mandela about whom a friend wrote:

i am the man you will never defeat
i will be your shadow, to be with
you always
and one day
when the sun rises
the shadow will move.
Mongane Serote

Graceland

Listen to the music of Paul Simon and Ladysmith Black Mambaza on the 'Graceland' album. You will learn much about the music and culture of Africa.

WOMEN AND DEVELOPMENT

Women are very important workers in African economies. According to the International Labour Organisation, women form $1/2$ of the world's population, $1/3$ of the official labour force and do nearly $2/3$ of the world's workhours. Yet they directly receive only $1/10$ of the world's income and own less than $1/100$ of the world's property. Try to explain these figures.

21 Changing patterns of industry

Christmas toys tell us much about new world industrial patterns. If we look at the toy-boxes and consider the continent where most of the producing countries are located, what pattern do we see? The continent is Asia and the countries are probably countries like Taiwan, Singapore and S. Korea. These are described as Newly Industrialised Countries (NICs).

Just as many developing countries of the world are beginning to change their industrial patterns, we can also notice changes taking place in the older, established centres of industry. Landscapes such as the Ruhr in Germany, South Wales and the North of England show many indications of industrial change and decline. Many of these older industrial landscapes have been badly damaged by the industries which employed so many people in the past. The landscapes are now said to suffer from industrial blight.

Steel works, Gwent, Wales

CHANGING IRISH INDUSTRY

Cork has long been recognised as a leading European port. Its deep-water harbour allows ships and tankers to come and go with their cargoes. The entrance to the harbour has been deepened and a new deep-water berth has been built at Ringaskiddy. Large boats can sail right up to the city quays. There, on a site beside the River Lee, the Ford Motor Company set up its first factory outside the USA. That was in the year 1917 and for several decades after that, Fords gave steady employment and good wages to thousands of Cork workers.

Next to Fords was the Dunlop Factory where tyres, tubes, rubber boots and golf balls were made. The shipping lanes in and out of Cork Harbour were busy. Ships were built and repaired at the Verolme Dockyard near Cobh, on the eastern shore of the harbour.

This great era of Cork industry came to an end in the early 1980s. Changing patterns of industry throughout the world meant that car-assembly, tyre-manufacturing and ship-building were no longer as profitable in Ireland. The Dunlop factory closed in 1983 and worse was to follow the next year when Fords closed their plant and the Verolme dockyard closed its gates for the last time. Cork city and the towns and villages around the harbour area entered a period of high unemployment and recession.

NEWER CORK INDUSTRIES

The gap left in the industrial life of Cork by the closing of the older industries has been filled by the growth and success in recent years of many chemical and computer industries. Let us look closely at these two areas of industrial growth.

THE CHEMICAL INDUSTRY

In previous *Worldwise* books we have looked at examples of pollution made by people. Like most human activities, the growth of the chemical industry in Ireland has had a number of problems. While the employment these new plants provide is very welcome, people rightly insist that protection of the environment is even more important.

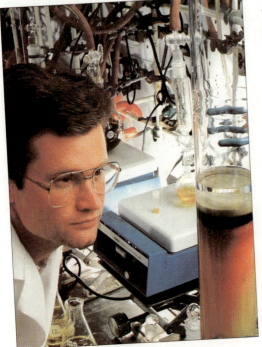

As well as making particular chemicals, the plant will often produce by-products which, if not properly treated, may be harmful to humans and/or to the environment.
The control of smells is often a problem.

Ireland is now among the top twelve chemical exporting nations in the world. The Pfizer Pharmaceutical Plant at Ringaskiddy in Co. Cork is the largest Pfizer plant outside the USA. Pfizer was one of a group of four companies in the USA to respond to a request from the US government in the early 1940s to develop a process to manufacture penicillin on a large scale. Ever since, the company has concentrated on discovering through research and then producing a wide range of pharmaceutical products.

Pfizer is one of the more important employers in the Cork area and has been in production since 1971. The major buildings consist of three large production plants, a large modern wastewater treatment plant and a modern laboratory building.
The manufactured bulk pharmaceuticals (medicines) are exported in large containers by sea to a central distribution point in Brussels. From there they are redirected to other plants by road, rail, sea or air. They are then converted into pills, capsules, and ointments, for worldwide distribution.

Pfizer also has bulk pharmaceutical plants in the USA similar to Ringaskiddy. These supply the American market. Worldwide, Pfizer employ around 40,000 people.

QUESTIONS

1. Name two Newly Industrialised Countries in Asia.
2. Why were companies such as Fords and Dunlops attracted to Cork?
3. What did Pfizer help to produce in the United States in the 1940s?
4. Why might Brussels have been chosen as a distribution centre for Pfizer products? Hint – centre.
5. Why are older, industrially-damaged landscapes often said to be blighted? (Hint – potato blight).

THE COMPUTER INDUSTRY

The manufacture of computers and other high-technology equipment is Cork's second major area of industrial growth. Many of the leading hi-tech companies from the U.S.A., Europe, Japan and Australia have established themselves in the region. Apple Computers, Bourns Electronics, Liebert International and Western Digital are but a few of Cork's new generation of employers. Thousands of young Irish people have found exciting employment with these companies.

The IDA (Industrial Development Authority) has helped to bring these electronic companies to the various industrial estates spread throughout the city. Cork Technology Park has been set up in the western suburbs. The National Micro-Electronics Centre is based in Cork and is attached to the local University College. NMEC carries out research in electronics and provides advice for both new and established electronics companies throughout Ireland.

Apple Computers Ltd. is one of the largest employers in Cork city. The plant, at Hollyhill Industrial Estate, was established in 1980. This major multinational company has a series of plants throughout the world. Apple in Cork manufacture the Apple and the Macintosh ranges of computers. From Cork they are distributed throughout Europe. There are now one million Macintosh computers in use in Europe, all made in Cork and using any of eighteen different European languages.

The European Service Centre is also located in the Cork plant. This means that all Macintosh and Apple units in need of repair are brought back to Cork for servicing. The company also manufactures hard disk drives, laser printers and printed circuit boards. Each of these developments is an example of ancillary industry.

QUESTIONS

1. Why are high-technology industries such attractive places to work in?
2. What attractions might Cork and other Irish sites offer to foreign companies?
3. Explain the term 'multinational company'.
4. Could you suggest any of the eighteen European languages which may be used in Macintosh computers.
5. Why do Macintosh use such a large number of languages?
6. An ancillary service industry is one that develops after the parent company grows and prospers. Name some of the ancillary services which Apple Computers have located in Cork city.
7. Can you explain why such strong links exist between the high-technology industries and groups like the National Micro-Electronics Centre?
8. Why did the decline of the older Cork industries result in a period of unemployment and recession?
9. Explain the term IDA and find out a little about its role in bringing industries to any area.
10. If there are any IDA developments in your area find out which industries have been attracted to your locality, what numbers of people are employed, what products are manufactured and which markets are supplied by the industries.

22 Land of the rising sun – Japan

Speaking of industry, as we were in our previous chapter, have you noticed how many Japanese cars there are on our streets and roadways? Do you know that many of the television sets, video-recorders and transistor radios in our homes have been imported from Japan? If you look in the window of a camera shop you will see many cameras and rolls of film marked 'Made in Japan'.

When it comes to the use of modern technology, the Japanese people are obviously among the world leaders. This makes Japan one of the most prosperous nations in the world today. Marco Polo described Japan as 'a wonderland of treasure'. We know it today as the 'Land of the Rising Sun' or sometimes as the 'Land of the Cherry Blossom'.

JAPAN

Japan consists of four main islands and almost 3,000 smaller ones. A string of islands like this is called an archipelago. The Japanese archipelago stretches in a roughly north-south direction for a distance of about 4,000km or eight times the length of Ireland.

Practically the entire population of 120 million people live on the four main islands – Honshu, Hokkaido, Shikoku and Kyushu. Over 80 per cent of these islands is mountainous and covered with dense forests. Farming land is very scarce – only about 15 per cent of the islands is suitable for farming. Farms are very small and no fertile land is let go to waste. Indeed, flat terraces are often carved out on the lower reaches of the hillsides to create extra land.

Tea shrubs and mulberry bushes are grown in these new fields – providing tea and silk for domestic use as well as for export. Lower down the valleys, rice is grown in paddy-fields and this is the main food of the Japanese people.

Because so much of Japan is mountainous and because there is such great demand for agricultural land, the entire population lives on a mere 3 per cent of the available space. This gives Japan one of the highest densities of population in the world and 80 per cent of Japan's population live in cities.

Mountain   Tree   Woman

A TURBULENT LAND

Japan lies where two of the plates of the earth's crust meet – the Pacific and the Eurasian plates. As a result of this, the country suffers from earthquakes, tidal waves and volcanic eruptions. The worst natural disaster in modern Japanese history was the Great Earthquake of 1923. The cities of Tokyo and Yokohama were destroyed, with the loss of 100,000 lives.

There are over seventy volcanoes in Japan, some of them dormant and others active. The string of volcanoes that lies along the Japanese archipelago is part of the great 'Ring of Fire' that circles the Pacific Ocean. The well-known Mt. Fuji, overlooking the city of Tokyo, is volcanic but has been dormant since 1707. It is a world-famous tourist attraction and is climbed by half a million people every year.

Typhoons hit Japan between June and October each year. Winds near the 'eye' of a typhoon can be ferocious and can cause dreadful damage to land and property. Tidal waves, 20 to 30 metres high, often accompany typhoons and batter the coastline of Japan. These tidal waves are called *tsunamis* and can travel at speeds of up to 100km an hour.

JAPAN'S PEOPLE

The Japanese are a very distinctive people, with their own language, their own alphabet, their own customs and a long, proud heritage. Japanese art is very delicate and very beautiful. The Japanese are extremely fond of flowers and plants and the country has many exquisite public gardens. These gardens often have streams, ponds, waterfalls and decorative bridges.

JAPAN AT WAR AND AT PEACE

Japan entered World War 2 on 7 December 1941 when it attacked the American navy base at Pearl Harbour in the Pacific Ocean, killing over 2,000 men. On 6 August 1945, the Americans dropped the first atomic bomb on the city of Hiroshima on the island of Honshu.

Three days later another atomic bomb was dropped on the city of Nagasaki on Kyushu. Many buildings in both cities were flattened and over 160,000 people were killed immediately. Thousands more died later from the radio-activity left behind by the bombs. On 14 August 1945 Japan surrendered and World War 2 was over – but at a dreadful cost. The economy of Japan was in ruins, just like its cities.

By hard work and sound planning the Japanese have built up their economy once again to become one of the wealthiest nations of the modern world.

> Typhoons are storms which can cause widespread damage in the tropical areas of the world. They are also called hurricanes or tropical storms. Typhoons are whirling storms of violent wind and rain. They can measure hundreds of kilometres across and can last for several hours. Every year weather forecasters begin by naming the first tropical storm with a name beginning with the letter A. The second storm is named with a B and so on. Every alternate name is that of a boy or girl. It's good to see equality!

JAPANESE INDUSTRY

The industrial exports of Japan vary from widely available consumer products, such as motor cars, to highly specialised scientific equipment. The Nissan Motor Company was established in Japan in 1933. It is now the world's fifth largest manufacturer of motor cars. The headquarters of Nissan Europe is located in Amsterdam. Like all other major motor companies, Nissan produces a wide range of models – ranging from large to small. Can you name any of the more popular Nissan cars used in Ireland?

The Nikon Camera company was established in Tokyo in 1917. Most of the photographs for the *Worldwise* series were taken with a Nikon camera made in Japan. These high-precision pieces of equipment show one of the greatest skills of the Japanese people – the ability to build reliable and reasonably priced equipment. They use technically advanced production methods. Nikon cameras were chosen by NASA as the main camera systems for the American space programme.

JAPANESE GARDENS

Tully House, a short distance from Kildare Stud was founded by Lord Wavertree in 1916. The gardens around the house are world famous. They were laid out in 1906 by Eito, a celebrated Japanese gardener. The gardens celebrate the different stages of life – from the cradle to the grave – which we go through as people.

TO DO

Here are the principal stages in the production of Nissan motor cars at the Oppoma Plant, on Tokyo Bay. Each stage represents part of the production process. We want you to take the stages and put them into a flow-diagram which will better illustrate the systems approach taken by Nissan cars.

1. **PLANNING:**
   The main features of a new car are discussed by the team.

2. **DESIGN:**
   All the data and measurements of the new car are worked out.

3. **SHAPING:**
   Automatic presses produce the main shapes of the car from sheets of metal.

4. **BODY ASSEMBLY:**
   This, and many other tasks on the assembly line, are done by welding robots. These machines can join up to seventy points at a time.

5. **PAINTING:**
   The car body is washed in a special liquid, dipped in a primer tank and then automatically sprayed with paint.

6. **TRIM LINE:**
   All the items made of leather, cloth, glass, etc. are added at this stage.

7. **ENGINE FITTING:**
   Car engines are made at the Yokohama Plant and brought to Oppoma for fitting to the new cars.

8. **FINAL CHECK:**
   A complete check is carried out on the entire car to ensure that everything works perfectly. It is even driven through a high-pressure shower.

9. **DISTRIBUTION:**
   As many as 50,000 finished cars are exported from Oppoma every month.

23 Going to the Americas

The Atlantic Ocean lies to the west of Ireland. If we cross this great seaway we will reach the Americas. These vast continents are made up of North, Central and South America.

CANADA

North America consists of three countries – Canada, the United States of America and Mexico. Most of Canada's population of 26 million people live close to its southern border and along the Canadian side of the St. Lawrence River. This vast sea-way connects the Great Lakes with the Atlantic Ocean, and ships can sail up past Quebec and Montreal and on to the large American cities of Detroit and Chicago. Montreal is the largest city in Canada and Ottawa is the capital.

The Eskimoes live in the far north of Canada. Many of them now live in towns and have normal jobs; others pursue the old ways of hunting and fishing. These Eskimoes use a kind of canoe, called a kayak – which is made of skins. In summer they live in tents and in winter they live in igloos, houses which are made of blocks of ice and are really warm inside.

Almost half of Canada is covered by forests – both coniferous and deciduous. The felling of trees and the manufacture of paper form the country's biggest industry. Trees that are cut down are replaced by young ones. There are many large paper mills along the river banks. The logs are floated down the rivers to the mills where they are first crushed into pulp and then made into paper. Canada is the world's largest producer of newsprint – the paper used for newspapers.

The treeless grassy plains of southern Canada are called prairies and they are one of the main wheat-producing areas of the world. The Canadian prairies are so vast that it takes a speeding train twenty-four hours to cross them. Fruit farms are quite common on the prairies also.

THE UNITED STATES OF AMERICA

The USA has fifty states, two of which – Alaska and Hawaii – are separated from the main group. The capital, Washington, is not in any state but is situated in a territory of its own, known as the District of Columbia. Each state makes its own laws but all of them are governed by the federal government in Washington. The President is head of the US government.

The US is a rich nation, with numerous industries, natural resources and vast farms. That is not to say that the USA is without poverty. Even under the shadow of the Capitol Building in Washington DC, some people live in dreadful slum conditions. Some minority peoples such as the native 'Indians' do not have much of the nation's wealth.

Most Americans work in the service industries – government departments, hospitals, banks, schools, radio, television, travel and tourism. Nearly 50 per cent of the land of the US is farmed, yet only 2 per cent of the working population are employed in agriculture. American farms are often huge ranches. These farms are highly organised and well equipped. Each American farmer can produce enough food for forty-five people.

Cotton, tobacco and sugar-cane are grown in the southern states. In the northern states, near the Canadian border, wheat and maize are grown extensively. The coastal strip of California, between the Rocky Mountains and the Pacific Ocean, is warm in winter and very hot in summer. Grapes, oranges and melons grow there. The San Andreas fault extends along the Californian coast. It is one of the largest cracks in the earth's crust, so this region is very prone to earthquakes.

In the Rocky Mountains, copper, lead and zinc are mined. Just east of the Rockies lie the hot barren deserts, like you see in 'Western' films. The Grand Canyon in Arizona was formed by the Colorado River cutting a vertical gorge down through a high rock plateau. Its spectacular views make the Grand Canyon a very popular tourist attraction. Further north in Wyoming, tourists flock to the Yellowstone National Park to see the geyser, Old Faithful, spurt its hot water forty metres up into the air. Yet another spectacular sight is that of the Niagara Falls on the border between USA and Canada.

In the southern tip of Florida lie the warm, humid swamps of the Everglades. This is a natural wonderland, teeming with some of the most colourful wildlife in the world – fish, birds, mammals and insects. The Everglades are now far smaller than they once were. Large areas have been destroyed to create land for building, roads and drainage.

The Statue of Liberty at the entrance to New York harbour

Mexico city: in search of left-overs amid the rubbish dumps

MEXICO

Mexico is a very mountainous country. Only the narrow coastal strips are low-lying. Most of the people live on the high central plateau. Mexico City, the capital, is the world's largest city and the oldest city in the Americas. It was founded by the Aztecs in the fourteenth century.

The central plateau is very rich in minerals – gold, copper and lead. The climate is suitable for plantations of coffee and maize. Maize, also known as Indian Corn, is the basic food of the Mexican people. Chicle, a sticky substance obtained from the Mexican forests, is the main substance used in the manufacture of chewing gum.

Map Work

1. Write down the names of the five Great Lakes that form part of the boundary between Canada and the USA. Note: Their initial letters make the word 'homes'.
2. On the shores of which lakes are the cities of Chicago and Detroit?
3. Between which two lakes are the Niagara Falls?
4. Name the huge bay that divides Canada almost in two.
5. Name three cities on or near the St. Lawrence River.
6. Where are the Appalachian Mountains?
7. In which states are Disneyland and Disney World?
8. The Mississippi and Missouri rivers drain the Great Plains of the USA. Near what city do they meet?
9. Which river forms part of the boundary between the USA and Mexico?
10. Through which North American countries do (a) the Arctic Circle and (b) the Tropic of Cancer run?

CENTRAL AMERICA

Central America is a long narrow strip of land between North and South America. Six of the seven countries were part of the Spanish Empire up to the 1920s. The Republic of Belize was formerly an English colony and became independent in 1981. English is still the official language of Belize. Spanish is spoken in the other Central American republics.

Unlike the USA and Canada, the countries of Central America are poor and under-developed. Civil wars have hindered the growth of their economies. They are also very subject to such natural disasters as earthquakes and hurricanes.

The Panama Canal, built by the Americans between 1904 and 1914, is still one of the busiest and most important canals in the world. It is sixty-four kilometres long and a line of ships makes its way through the canal in one direction at a time.

The West Indies are a group of islands in the Caribbean Sea. They extend in an archipelago from Cuba, off the tip of Florida, to Trinidad, off the coast of Venezuela. Sugar-cane and tobacco are the chief products of the islands.

Map Work

1. Name the six Spanish-speaking countries of Central America.
2. Which Central American countries are nearest the Tropic of Cancer?
3. What great oceans are linked by the Panama Canal?
4. A ship sailing from San Francisco to New York can take a short-cut through the Panama Canal. Otherwise it would have to travel south around Cape Horn. How many times longer would this journey be than the Panama route? Use a ruler and a divider to measure the distance.
5. Name the capital of each of the seven Central American countries.
6. Which North American country shares a border with Central America?
7. Which South American country shares a border with Central America?
8. Which island is the largest of the West Indies?
9. What country shares an island with Haiti?
10. On what island is Kingston?

SOUTH AMERICA - NATIVE PEOPLES

People had lived on the American continent for thousands and thousands of years before the Europeans became aware of its existence. The first settlers made their way there from northern Asia. They crossed over the land bridge that once joined Asia to Alaska. Some of them stayed in the north of America and were the ancestors of today's Eskimoes. Other tribes gradually made the long journey south to Mexico, and to Central and South America.

The Aztecs of Mexico were fierce and dreaded warriors who conquered and terrorised other native peoples. Yet they practised writing, mathematics, art and craftwork.

The Mayas lived in what is now Central America and the southern part of Mexico. They made their own calendar and invented their own form of hieroglyphic writing. What brought the powerful Mayan Empire to an end remains a mystery – they just ceased to be, leaving only a heap of ruined buildings.

The richest and best organised of the native civilizations was the Inca Kingdom of South America. They lived in the high Andes mountains roughly where Peru is now. At one time more than fifteen million Incas lived there. The ruins of Machu Picchu give some idea of the splendour of the Inca Kingdom.

All these peoples were Asian in origin. When the Europeans came, thinking they had sailed west around the world to India, they called these natives Indians. They proceeded to slaughter and rob them in the name of conquest. To the Europeans this was a New World. To their shame, it was also the destruction of an Old World.

THE COLONIES OF SOUTH AMERICA

Spinning wool in the highlands of Bolivia

'In fourteen hundred and ninety-two, Columbus sailed the ocean blue.' From that date onwards the race to colonise the New World was on. Portuguese explorers captured Brazil and claimed it for their own country. Amerigo Vespucci, an Italian sailing for the Spanish crown, charted the east coast of South America in 1497. It was after Amerigo that the new continent was names, and not after Columbus who first discovered it.

The Aztec Kingdom of Mexico fell to Hernando Cortez and that of the Incas fell to Francisco Pizzaro. Both of these plunderers were Spaniards and nearly all of the wondrous treasures of the 'Indians' were shipped back to the royal court in Spain. The Spaniards colonised most of South America and Spanish remains the main language of the region to this day. Portuguese is the official language of Brazil.

The southern tip of the continent remained in native hands. When, in 1520, Ferdinand Magellan sailed through the straits that bear his name, he saw the lights of the fires lit by the natives on the island to the south and so he called it *Tierro del Fuego* – The Land of Fire.

QUESTIONS

1. Where does the name America come from?
2. Spanish explorers, having made the long voyage across the Atlantic, were glad to notice fresh westerly winds blowing off the land. 'These are good airs,' they said and they named the settlement they founded in Argentina 'Good Airs'. By what name do we know it?
3. A look-out high on the mast of a ship shouted to those on deck below that he could see a mountain ahead. Indeed he could, and the settlement they founded in Uruguay got its name from that first glimpse of land. What is that city called?
4. Where did the ancient Incas live?
5. What ancient kingdoms were destroyed by Cortez and Pizzaro?
7. Whose journey did Tim Severin re-enact when he crossed the Atlantic in a currach?
8. Why do people like Severin and Heyerdahl travel the world on voyages of discovery and exploration?
9. If you had your choice, what journey or voyage made by a great explorer would you re-enact? Explain your choice.
10. Can you name any parts of the world which still remain relatively unexplored and await proper mapping and investigation?

SOUTH AMERICA TODAY

The land of South America is rich in oil, tin and copper. Yet there is great poverty and want in all of its countries. South American governments are often unstable and sometimes military groups take over control of countries by force.

Most people live in cities or towns. Sao Paulo, Rio de Janeiro and Buenos Aires are among the ten largest cities of the world. A typical South American city can have skyscrapers, factories and high-rise apartments in the city centre while shanty-towns sprawl along the outer suburbs. As more and more people come into the cities from the countryside, conditions in the shanty-towns become worse.

Every year a fantastic carnival of colour, dance and music is held in Rio. Soccer is the major sport of most South American countries. South America is home to a huge variety of climates and landscapes, ranging from the hot tropical forests of Brazil to the dry arid desert of Atacama, where little grows.

South American Quiz Time

Everybody in class has to make out a question for a quiz on South America. You can include the countries, capitals, borders, etc.

Look as well at the wider picture, e.g.
- How many countries touch Brazil?
- What South American countries do not have a border with the sea?
- Which three South American countries does the equator pass through?

When everybody has their questions completed pass them to your teacher. All of the questions will be attempted by each pupil and whoever gets most questions correct will win the quiz.

24 Passage to India

When you think of India, what images of that country come to your mind? Do you recall the great love of Mother Teresa for the homeless and the dying on the streets of Calcutta? Perhaps you have seen the film of the life of Gandhi and how in 1946 he peacefully led the people of India to independence from Britain.

You may have seen pictures of Hindu pilgrims making their way to the River Ganges, there to bathe themselves in its holy waters. The Indian Elephant, carrying passengers on its back through the crowded streets and the Bengal tiger with its vivid yellow stripes are two more striking images of India.

QUESTIONS

Use the map on Page 118 and your atlas for help in answering these questions.
1. What shape has India?
2. What ocean lies to the south?
3. Name the bay that lies to the east.
4. What sea is west of India?
5. What large island lies off the south coast of India?
6. Name the strait that separates this island from India.
7. What is the capital city of India?
8. Name the countries that border India.
9. What great river flows across the north of India and into the Bay of Bengal?

LOOKING AT INDIA

What is it really like, this vast country which is home to more than 800 million people? Because it covers such a huge area of land, India has many varied landscapes ranging from the icy snow-covered mountains in the north to the green tropical grasslands along the south coast. It has one of the oldest civilisations in the world and the cultures of its people are as varied as the landscape itself.

RELIGIONS

Most Indian people are Hindus and have their own religious beliefs and customs. They worship many gods including the River Ganges and Brahma, their supreme god. A Hindu is born into one of four social groups or castes. Each caste (except the unfortunate people in the lowest caste), is considered superior to those below it. Hindus believe in reincarnation. They do not eat meat and to them the cow is a sacred animal. Even in cities and towns, cows are allowed to wander at will.

About one in ten of the people of India is a Muslim. Their religion, known as Islam, was founded by the prophet Mohammed. The sayings and prophesies of Mohammed are written down in the Muslim's holy book – The Koran.

In Northern India, some people are Buddhist. In the mountains and valleys of the Himalayas there are many exotic temples to honour the founder Buddha, who lived in Northern India abuot 500 years BC. Elsewhere in India there are splendid Muslim mosques. These have tall narrow towers called minarets, from the top of which the followers of Mohammed are called to worship several times each day.

Unfortunately the different peoples of what we call the Indian 'subcontinent' have often fought over their religious differences. In 1947 the people of India, under the leadership of Mahatma Gandhi, demanded their freedom from Britain. The subcontinent was divided along religious lines. India became a mostly Hindu state while Pakistan was established for the Muslims.

Pakistan was in two parts, about 1,500km apart. West Pakistan bordered India to the north-west and East Pakistan was established in the north-east. In 1971 East Pakistan broke away to form an independent state and became known as Bangladesh. The other region is now known as Pakistan.

Since gaining its independence, India has developed its economy quickly and its people now produce enough food to feed the entire population. Furthermore, it is now the tenth most industrialised nation in the world. Most Indians live on a diet of rice, vegetables and fruit.

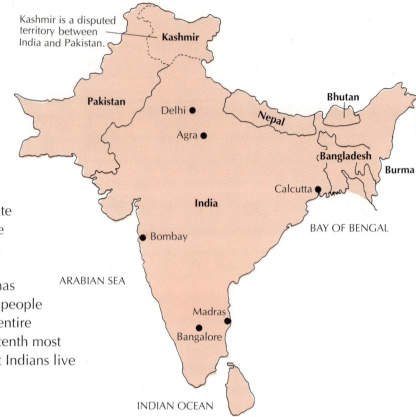

Kashmir is a disputed territory between India and Pakistan.

INDIAN LANDSCAPES

The Himalaya mountain range extends from Kashmir near the border with Pakistan to the state of Assam, north of the Bay of Bengal. Here are some of the highest mountains in the world, with several peaks over 7,500 metres high. The highest mountain in the world (8,848m) is on the border between Nepal and Tibet.

The Himalayas form a massive natural barrier between India and the rest of Asia, with travel possible only through a few passes in the snow-covered mountains. Sometimes these passes are closed by landslides or avalanches. The mountain scenery here on 'The Roof of the World' is magnificent.

THE RIVER PLAINS

The valley of the Ganges, together with the valleys of the Indus and the Brahmaputra, form a large stretch of rich alluvium land. The land is very flat. The Ganges Plain is one of the most densely populated areas on earth. About one-third of the people of India live there. To the millions who live along its banks, and to all Hindu people everywhere, Mother Ganges is the goddess of Life and Death.

Indian legend says that the Ganges fell from Heaven. Hindu pilgrims come from afar to bathe in its sacred waters. This, they believe, washes away all trace of sin. To bathe in the Ganges and then to die, to have one's body cremated and the ashes scattered on the water, is the surest guarantee of entry to Heaven.

Every morning, even before daybreak, throngs of Hindus gather along the river bank and the first ray of sunlight from the east finds them washing, floating, swimming and paddling in the river. Because there are over 100 cities along its banks, with very little treatment of sewage, the Ganges has become severely polluted.

THE PENINSULA OF INDIA

You will see from the map that the peninsula of India is shaped like a triangle. Most of it is hilly or at least of high altitude. The Western Ghats Mountains and the Eastern Ghats Mountains form two sides of the triangle, with the high ground of the Deccan Plateau in between. There are often narrow stretches of tropical coastline between the Ghats and the sea, their golden beaches fringed with waving palms.

As in many parts of the world you can see great poverty and great wealth side by side. Some members of the Indian upper caste lead a life of luxury undreamed of in the West. Meanwhile there are over a million homeless on the steets of Calcutta. Jute, which is used in the manufacture of sacks and cloth, is grown in the region west of Calcutta. There are large tea-plantations in the southern part of the peninsula.

DELHI

Delhi, the capital of India, is really two cities in one. New Delhi has wide tree-lined streets with modern shopping centres and office apartments. Inside the walls of Old Delhi the narrow streets are lined with tiny shops and bazaars. Local artists make leather and brass works of art while buyers wait.

Outside on the streets the calls of animals and the cries of the sellers fill the air. Everyone bargains about the price before buying something in a bazaar.

QUESTIONS

1. What mountains cut India off from the rest of Asia?
2. What is the highest peak in the range?
3. Who was the first person to climb the highest mountain in the world?
4. What are the religious followers of Mohammed called?
5. Who was the founder of Buddhism?
6. Which is the major religion of India?
7. Gandhi preached peaceful resistance to British rule. Was his campaign successful?
8. What was the old name for Bangladesh?
9. Each year between June and September the delta of the Ganges is swept with torrential rains. They are vital for the agriculture of the region but sometimes they cause severe flooding. What are these summer rains called?
10. At Agra, just south of Delhi, stands a magnificent white marble building that was built by a seventeenth-century Emperor in memory of his wife. It is one of the great tourist attractions of the world and is really magical when seen by moonlight. What is it called?

Cities

Can you name these Indian cities? Their letters are a little mixed up!

MYBBOA
RAAG
AADSMR
ERALBGNAO
ACLUCTAT
LEIHD

25 Life down under

Sometimes we say that Australians live 'down under'. Australia is very far away from us, on the other side of the globe. When we have daylight, it is night-time in Australia. When we have summer, it is winter in the southern hemisphere. It is not unusual for Australian families to spend Christmas Day picnicing on a beach under the hot summer sun.

THE NATIVE AUSTRALIANS

Australia has been inhabited by people for far longer than Ireland has. The first settlers in Australia were called 'Aborigines'. They crossed over to the island continent from the mainland of Asia. For thousands upon thousands of years, their descendants and the new waves of settlers lived a primitive hunting life in what is, for the most part, a dry and barren country.

It was only about 400 years ago that the first European explorers came to Australia. In 1606 a Spaniard named de Torres sailed through the strait between Australia and Papua New Guinea. We now call this stretch of water Torres Strait. Ten years later, Hartog, a Dutch sea-captain made the first recorded landing of a European explorer on Australian soil. His fellow countryman, Tasman, discovered the vast island off the south coast which he called Van Diemen's Land.

These early European explorers were not greatly impressed by the dry desert lands of the north and west of the new country. It was not until Captain James Cook explored eastern Australia in 1770 that the British realised how valuable these new lands could be. On his return journey from an expedition to Tahiti, Cook sailed along the east coast of Australia and charted the bays and the headlands as he went. He landed at a place rich in plants and flowers, which he named Botany Bay and which is today a suburb of the city of Sydney.

As a result of Cook's explorations, Britain claimed Australia as a colony and used it as a place of imprisonment for thousands of convicts and political prisoners. In all, about 160,000 of Britain's unwanted were shipped out there, the voyage made under dreadful and cruel conditions. Many died on the high seas, during the eight-month voyage.

Of this number about 45,000 were Irish. Leaders of the Young Ireland rebellion of 1848 and of the Fenian Rising in 1867 were transported across the world to concentration camps in Van Diemen's Land and Botany Bay. Some escaped to America. Others served their sentence and settled down to a life of farming in Australia. Today a large part of Australia's population is of British or Irish descent.

123

LIFE IN THE OUTBACK

Nowadays about two-thirds of the Aboriginal people live in towns and cities. But many still live in small tribes in the dry barren centre of the country – what Australians call 'the outback'. An Aboriginal hunter can tell from looking at the ground what animals have recently passed that way. The most famous weapon of the Aborigines is the boomerang. When thrown skilfully it will zoom back again to the hunter if it does not strike its target on the way.

Aborigines lighting a fire

When the European settlers arrived in Australia 200 years ago they found an Aboriginal population numbering 300,000 before them. As the white settlers moved in from the coastal settlements in search of new farming lands, they were often very cruel to the Aborigines who stood in their way.

The Australian government today tries to preserve the Aboriginal way of life and indeed the Aboriginal population is growing once again. There are still less Aborigines than there were 200 years ago. The population of European stock has grown to 16 million.

Australia has always encouraged emigration and in particular has given a new home to refugees forced to flee from other countries. Since World War 2 about half a million refugees and displaced people have settled down to a new life in Australia.

AUSTRALIA

Australia is one of the most urbanised countries in the world. About 70 per cent of the population live in the 10 largest cities – most of which are on the south-east coast. The combined population of the cities of Sydney and Melbourne is 6 million people.

Many of the industries in the large cities are based on the farm produce of the countryside. Its warm climate makes Australia a top fruit-producing country. Fresh fruit and tinned fruit are exported to many parts of the world. Wheat, wool, meat, sugar, poultry and dairy produce are other major exports. Japan is the main purchaser of Australian exports.

About half the area of the Australian continent is given over to sheep rearing. Scattered through the outback are huge sheep-stations or farms, so big that it would take an entire day for the sheep-farmer to drive around the boundaries of the station. At any time, there are probably about 16 million sheep in Australia. It is the world's largest producer of wool.

QUESTIONS AND MAP WORK

Use your atlas for some help to answer these questions.

1. Why was Australia so attractive as a place to which the British government could transport its convicts and political prisoners?
2. Why is Australia so attractive today for emigrants?
3. With what sport do you associate the team known as the 'Wallabies'?
4. What are the national colours of Australia?
5. Why were the Aborigines so badly treated by early European settlers?
6. What could the Australian government do to guarantee equality for the Aboriginal population?
7. Australia is divided into six states and two territories. The capital city is located in the smaller of the territories (Australian Capital Territory). What is the capital of Australia?
8. The larger of the territories, in the north of the country, achieved self-government in 1978. What is it called?
9. Name the five mainland states.
10. Which state is an island?
11. Name the six state capitals.
12. What is the name of the chain of coral islands that lie off the north-east coast of Australia?
13. The largest rock in the world stands splendidly in the centre of Australia. What is it called?
14. Which long range of mountains (3,000km) stretches from the Gulf of Carpentaria in the north to Bass Strait in the south?

What am I?

1. I am a wild Australian dog. I have a yellowish brown coat and some people say I look like a wolf. What am I?
2. I am a grey furry animal and I live up on the eucalyptus tree feeding on its leaves. What am I?
3. I am an egg-laying mammal. I have webbed feet, a bill like a duck's and a furry coat. What am I?
4. I have powerful hind legs that help me to leap along at great speed. I carry my young in my pouch. What am I?
5. I look like a pheasant and when I display my beautifully-coloured tail it looks like a musical instrument. What am I?

125

6 I can live in or out of the water. With my huge jaws and pointed teeth I can grab a horse from the shore and drag it under the water. What am I?
7 I am the second largest bird in the world – next to the ostrich – but I cannot fly. I am grey or brown in colour and I can run very fast on my three-toed feet. What am I?

NEW ZEALAND

New Zealand, which consists of two large islands and some smaller ones, lies about 2,000km south-east of Australia. As in the case of Australia, there was also a native population in New Zealand before European settlers arrived. The natives of New Zealand are called Maoris.

The Maoris have their own traditional costume, their own songs and music, and their own art forms. In modern times many Maoris live in towns and take a full part in the commerce and industry of their country. New Zealand is about three times the size of Ireland but its population is about the same as ours.

The climate of New Zealand is very like that of Ireland. Like ourselves, New Zealanders produce high-quality dairy produce. New Zealand butter is famous all over the world. Along the coast there are extensive sheep and cattle farms. Wool and meat are exported in large quantities.

At Rotorua on North Island and at other places throughout New Zealand there are many hot springs and geysers. A geyser is a spring that shoots jets of hot water into the air at intervals. Find out more about these interesting natural features, especially the one they call 'Old Faithful'.

QUESTIONS

1 Name the two chief islands of New Zealand.
2 What stretch of water separates them?
3 What is the capital of New Zealand?
4 The largest city is Auckland. On which island is it?
5 What name is given to the New Zealand rugby team?
6 Before a game they perform a haka. What is that?
7 I live only in New Zealand. I am a flightless bird with a long pointed beak. My brown feathers look like hair. My picture is one of the two national emblems of New Zealand. What am I?
8 We have learned where Torres Strait, Bass Strait and Cook Strait are. Use your atlas to find the names of the straits between the land masses in this box:

England — France
Spain — Morocco
Italy — Sicily
Sardinia — Corsica
India — Sri Lanka
Sumatra — Malay Peninsula
Korea — Japan
China — Taiwan
Alaska — Russia
Chile — Tierra del Fuego

26 *I'd like to see under the sea*

This year, and during the other years you studied *Worldwise* with us, we have spent most of our time looking at that part of planet earth which is dry land. And yet 70 per cent of the earth's surface is covered by water!

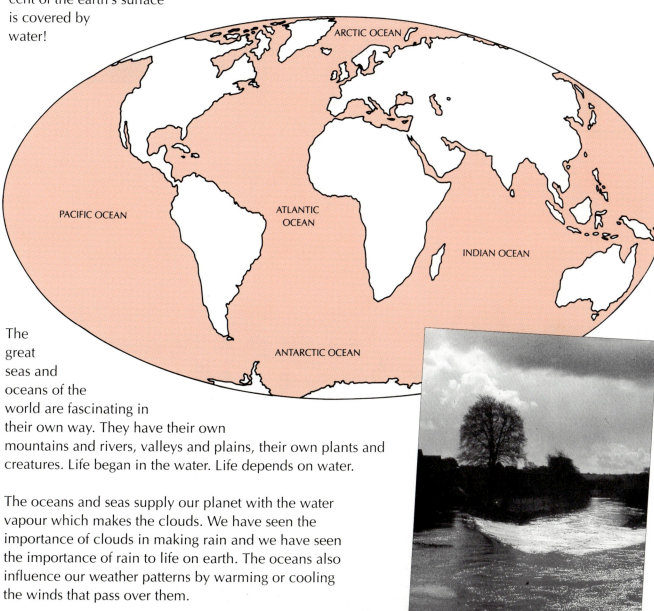

The great seas and oceans of the world are fascinating in their own way. They have their own mountains and rivers, valleys and plains, their own plants and creatures. Life began in the water. Life depends on water.

The oceans and seas supply our planet with the water vapour which makes the clouds. We have seen the importance of clouds in making rain and we have seen the importance of rain to life on earth. The oceans also influence our weather patterns by warming or cooling the winds that pass over them.

THE SEABED

The depth of the oceans varies from place to place. Where the continental plates meet there are many deep trenches. The Marianas Trench in the Pacific Ocean is the deepest part of the earth's sea. It is over 11km deep. On the other hand there are undersea mountains, some of which stick their heads over the sea surface.

Many such islands, especially in the Pacific and Indian Oceans, are volcanic. When these volcanoes are active, the lava thrown up can cause the island to grow wider and higher. In 1963, off the coast of Iceland, a new volcanic island sprang up to a height of 200 metres above sea level in just ten days.

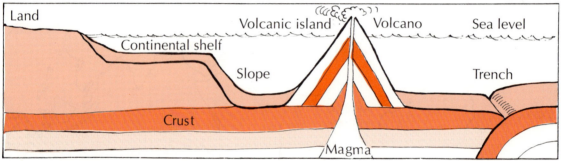

A continental shelf might be only about 350 metres deep. Beyond that, the average depth of the sea on the ocean floor is 4,000 metres. What does this tell us about the continental slope?

Clearing up the beaches of Saudi Arabia after the Gulf War oil spillage

QUESTIONS

1. What is the height of the earth's highest mountain?
2. What is the depth of the earth's deepest trench?
3. Work out the distance from the highest point to the lowest point.
4. Name the 5 main oceans of the world.
5. Which of the oceans is circled by the great volcanic 'Ring of Fire'?
6. What country suffers from tidal waves called 'tsunamis'?
7. This pie chart shows the relative volume of water in each of the five main oceans. List them in order of size.
8. There are, of course, many smaller seas on planet earth. Use your atlas to find out which seas are linked by:
   (a) The Panama Canal
   (b) The Suez Canal
   (c) Bering Strait
   (d) Strait of Gibraltar

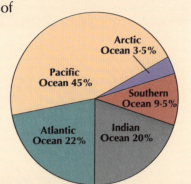

OCEAN CURRENTS

Currents are like rivers of warm or cold water moving through the sea. Some of them move on the surface; others deep down in the ocean. Currents can be as warm as 30°C or as cold as -2°C, depending on where they come from.

These currents can have a great influence on the countries that they touch. We in Ireland get the benefit of the warm North Atlantic Drift, also known as the Gulf Stream. This makes our climate milder than it would otherwise be.

Whaling ships use harpoon guns to wound the whales.

Sometimes we can find litter washed up on our beaches that has been brought there by currents. Pollution in one country can be carried by currents on to the shores of another. This shows once again, and we must never forget it, that planet earth is one single ecosystem.

Where warm currents and cold currents meet, heavy fog can occur. This can happen off the coast of Newfoundland, where the cold Labrador Current meets the warm Gulf Stream.

Dolphins in deep ocean

TO DO

Many atlases contain a map of the ocean currents. Use your map to find out where the earth's currents are. Make two lists – one of the warm currents and one of the cold ones.

LIFE IN THE SEA

There is an amazing abundance of life in the sea. All kinds of animal life occur there, including mammals. There are over 20,000 kinds of fish in the sea but there are double that number of molluscs (soft-bodied animals like oysters and mussels).

As on land, the animals of the sea depend on plants for life. There are billions of tiny microscopic plants floating around in the sea, often carried here and there by the ocean currents.

131

As with land plants, these sea plants use sunlight to produce oxygen in the water. Indeed, about 70 per cent of the oxygen in the earth's atmosphere originated in the seas.

The shallow continental shelves support many kinds of sea-weeds and plants. Deeper down in the oceans, beyond the continental slopes, the sunlight does not penetrate so there are less plants to be found.

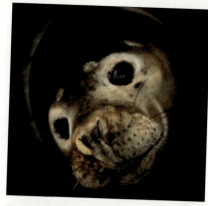

A seal covered in oil after an oilspill near the Shetland Islands

OCEAN LAYERS

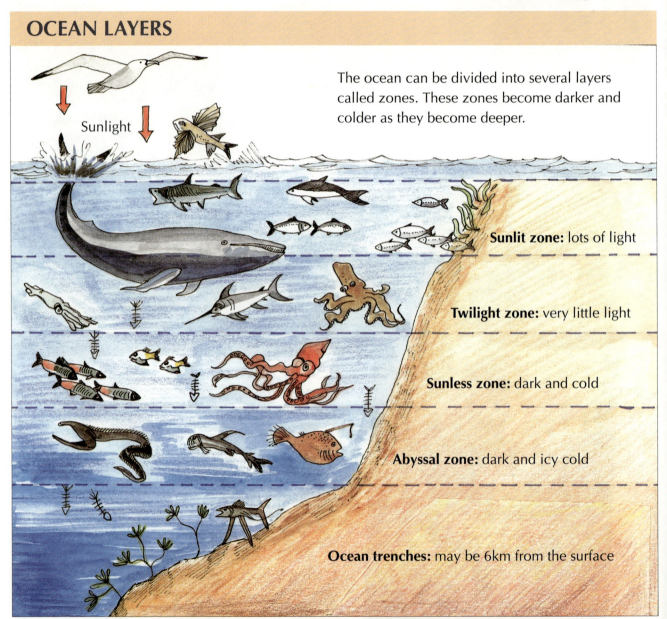

The ocean can be divided into several layers called zones. These zones become darker and colder as they become deeper.

Sunlit zone: lots of light

Twilight zone: very little light

Sunless zone: dark and cold

Abyssal zone: dark and icy cold

Ocean trenches: may be 6km from the surface

Our artist has drawn a picture of the ocean layers for you to study.

27 And on to Asia

The ancient Greeks who lived in the eastern Mediterranean knew only of three continents. Africa lay to the south, *Ereb* to the west and *Acu* to the east. *Ereb*, or Europe, was the land of the setting sun while *Acu*, or Asia, was the land of the rising sun.

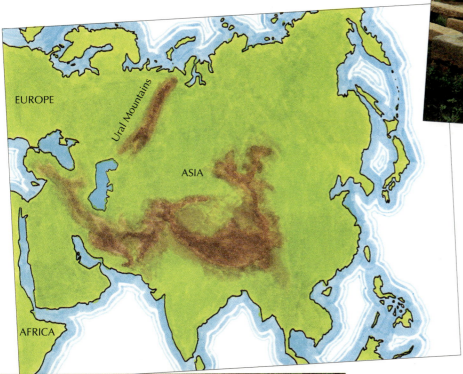

INTO ASIA

The continents of Europe and Asia form the landmass of Eurasia. If we journeyed from Europe to Asia how would we know we had gone from one continent to another? The traditional border between Europe and Asia is the Ural Mountain range. Europe lies west of the Urals while Asia lies to the east. As we shall see later, there are also cultural differences between the two continents.

ASIA IN HISTORY

China viewed from outer space

Papyrus

PAPER
We take paper for granted. Newspapers, books and schoolbooks give us so much information and pleasure. The word 'paper' comes from 'papyrus'. Papryus reeds were used by the ancient Egyptians to make a writing surface. We owe the invention of paper as we know it to the Chinese. In 105 a.D. T'sai Lun became the first known paper-maker.

It is thought that people have lived in Asia for at least 500,000 years. Archaeologists have found human remains in China and Java which supports this date.

The earliest known civilisations, located in the valley of the Tigris and Euphrates, developed in Western Asia between 500 and 300 B.C. Cities and trade, along with a primitive system of writing, were first found in Asia. Other great contributions to world learning by Asian people included the alphabet, the invention of the decimal system and knowledge about astronomy and medicine.

Part of the Great Wall of China

There has long been trade between Europe and Asia. Asian exports, such as herbs, spices and silks, have been popular in Europe since the early Middle Ages.

134

ASIA TODAY

Asia is the largest of the continents, covering just under one-third of the world's land surface. Over half the world's people live in Asia.

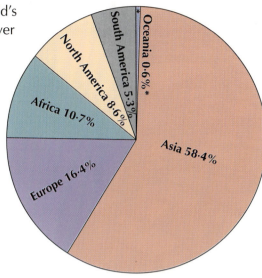
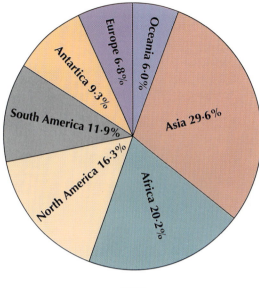

POPULATION

AREA

Asians and Europeans differ from each other in their racial characteristics, languages and religions.

In the past, major differences existed in the types of economy found in these continents. Traditionally, European economies have been more industrialised. European agriculture is very intensive and produces surpluses which are sold in markets.

Asian economies were less industrialised but that situation is now changing. New patterns of industry are developing in many Asian countries. Their agricultural systems are now producing very adequate levels of food. The many Asian famines throughout history are now largely a thing of the past.

QUESTIONS

1. Where does the word Asia come from and what is its meaning?
2. What is the traditional border between Europe and Asia?
3. How long are people thought to have lived in Asia?
4. Name some of the major contributions made by Asians to world learning.
5. Where does the word 'paper' come from?
6. Which continents cover (a) the greatest and (b) the least surface areas?
7. What percentage of the world's population lives in Asia?
8. Which continent has the smallest percentage of the world's population?

ASIATRAIL

Let's travel the Asiatrail. Use your atlas to find the names of the countries which our artist has numbered from 1- 44 on the map.

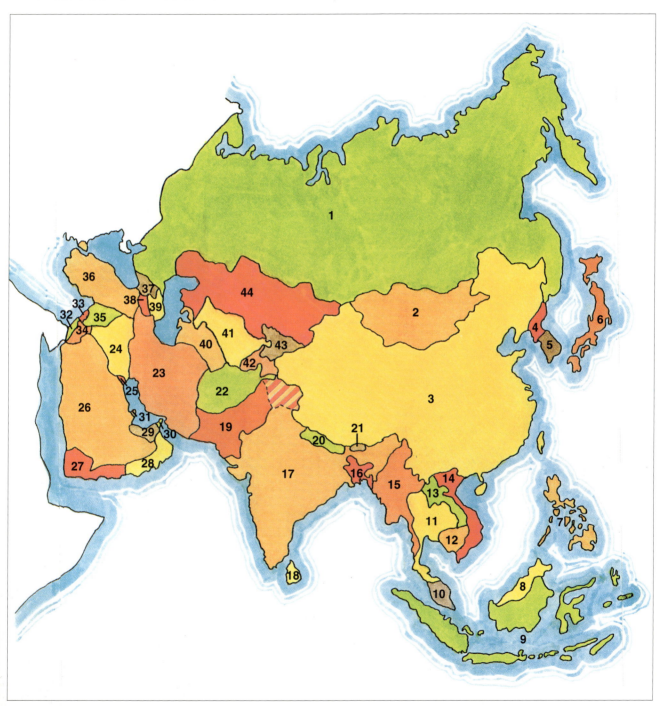

28 Understanding boundaries

These lines tell road users how they may or may not behave. They also act as boundaries. This means that they separate different spaces or territories from each other. You are already aware of other examples of boundaries. Have you all played picky or hopscotch at some stage? These street games really do illustrate boundaries – one foot in the wrong direction or the wrong space and … sorry, you're out!

RURAL AND URBAN BOUNDARIES

The outside walls of our homes act as boundaries. They tell people about the private space which is so important in all of our lives. They also guarantee us personal shelter and security. Rural dwellers have far less difficulty in preserving these aspects of their lives. There is so much more space available in the countryside and we can see that clearly in the photograph on top of p. 139. Our artist has drawn the principal boundaries on the sketch map beside it so you won't have any difficulty identifying them.

138

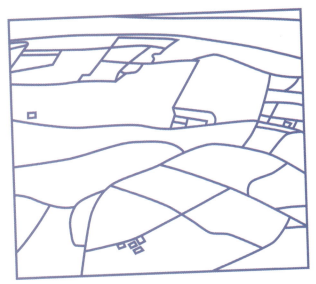

QUESTIONS

1. Name any five field-games which have boundaries (lines) as part of their rules.
2. Name any five board-games in which boundaries play an important part.
3. Why do people living in rural areas generally have greater privacy than urban dwellers?
4. Why is it important that we respect the rights of others in observing property boundaries? Could such boundaries ever be unfair to the general public? (Hint – closing traditional rights of way).
5. Draw a simple sketch map of your own home or locality showing some important boundaries.
6. Have a class quiz to see if you can list the counties of Ireland.

LARGE-SCALE BOUNDARIES

Maps which show units of territory such as counties or countries are called political maps. In the case of Irish counties, we will not find the boundaries marked on the ground. By and large, however, we can be on the look-out for reminders which tell us we have gone from one county into another. The road surface may change – usually only in colour – indicating that two distinct local authorities (called County Councils or Corporations) have responsibility for providing the services within their own boundaries. Another very useful indicator of county boundaries is the presence of a welcoming road-sign.

The people who originally drew our county boundaries sometimes used physical features as natural divisions between counties. Rivers and mountain ranges acted as natural separations between people when transport systems were not as advanced or as sophisticated as they are today.

These natural divisions also had a second attraction for map-makers. They were often thinly populated so there were relatively few people whose feelings might be upset by being in one unit as opposed to another.

It's a very interesting exercise to look at a political map of Ireland side-by-side with a map showing physical features, in order to identify natural boundaries between Irish counties.

INTERNATIONAL BOUNDARIES

It is possible to drive between two Irish counties, say Galway and Clare, without being alerted that one has crossed the county border. This situation does not generally apply in the case of going from one country to another. We usually have to show our passports and may even have to produce a special document – called a visa – which entitles us to enter a particular country.

These transactions will take place at a crossing-point on the international boundary. Quite often, people refer to the narrow belt of territory which separates countries as a frontier. Again, it's a very interesting exercise to see how some of the world's great rivers and mountain ranges act as international frontiers.

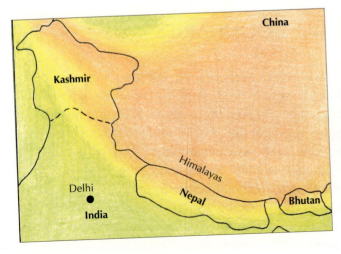

Looking down on the Himalaya Mountains from outer space

QUESTIONS

1. What is a political map?
2. How might you be aware you had crossed from one Irish county into another?
3. Mountain ranges and rivers were quite often used as natural boundaries. Why were they felt to be very suitable divisions between units of territory?
4. What is a visa?
5. Use your atlases to check which countries have the following physical features as parts of their international frontiers. In each case, we indicate whether the feature is a mountain range (M), a river (R) or a lake (L). Pyrénées (M), Himalayas (M), Alps (M), Andes (M), Rhine (R), Oder (R), Rio Grande (R), Ganges (R), Great Lakes (L) and Lake Tanganyika (L).

BOUNDARIES IN OUR MINDS

After the Second World War the continent of Europe was divided into two blocs. Eastern European countries were controlled by the USSR and followed a communist political system. The governments of Western European countries offered much more freedom to their peoples.

The frontier where these blocs met within central Europe became known as The Iron curtain. The city of Berlin was divided by a towering wall. Many people lost their lives while trying to escape across this wall to freedom. The Iron Curtain divided people from each other and became a boundary within minds as well as being a physical division.

It remained so until 1989 when, because of the foresight and the inspiration of President Mikhail Gorbachev, the people of Eastern European countries broke free. Germany was re-united. People were allowed to travel as they wished. The people who had been enclosed by boundaries and frontiers for many years were at last free. It was one of the most marvellous examples of how the human spirit cannot be enslaved by tyrants and can eventually overcome very many obstacles to freedom.

To Do

Why is it so important that we try to avoid creating boundaries in our minds? You might consider looking at the human rights of any minority – one in Ireland if you wish – and the ways in which our own very definite ideas are often unfair and wrong.

29 The world family

LIVING TOGETHER AND HELPING EACH OTHER

During our four years of *Worldwise* Geography we have voyaged far and wide throughout our world. Our starting point was our own local area and we returned on many occasions to look at the places in which we live. On a broader scale, we looked at planet earth and its place in the universe.

Our world is a place of contrast. Great beauty and splendour can be found side by side with problems of abject poverty and injustice. You will have the joy and the sadness of seeing such beauty and problems as you grow through adulthood.

THE WORLD FAMILY

Planet earth is just a tiny fraction of our universe. So too, we as individual beings form just a small part of the human race. What matters is not our size or our importance but our sharing a common humanity. Our individuality and our special place in the love and affection of family and friends are sources of joy and support.

142

TO SAY 'GOODBYE!'

We hope you have enjoyed reading and studying the *Worldwise* Geography series. To say a special goodbye, we have asked some famous people to give you their advice and photographs. Enjoy their words and your lives. Be worldwise and be happy!

ALICE TAYLOR

Alice is a wonderfully talented and relaxed writer who is very much at ease with her life. Her first major book, *To School Through The Fields*, tells of her childhood in a rural Ireland which has largely disappeared. It is important that we all retain our memories which may someday be an important part of folk memory and culture. Why not keep your own diary?

'Take time to get to know the people and place where you live now. Enjoy the everyday things around you.'

Change

The summer
still hangs
heavy and sweet
with sunlight
as it did last year

The autumn
still comes
showering gold and crimson
as it did last year.

The winter
still stings
clean and cold and white
as it did last year.

The spring
still comes
like a whisper
in the dark night.

It is only I
who have changed.

Charlotte Zolotow

GAY BYRNE

Everybody in Ireland knows Gay Byrne. As the presenter of the enormously popular 'Late Late Show' on television and his own Radio Show, he has continually used his skills to communicate with people. His gift of communication is a rare one and provdes us with a perfect example of talent and dedication being used in a career.

'You are the future citizens of Ireland and the world. Believe in yourselves, your talents and your skills.

JOAN BLACKBURN

Joan Blackburn has an honours degree in Physics. She is part of the team which works in the Central Forecasting Office (CFO) in the Meteorological Headquarters in Glasnevin. Her work involves analysing charts, computer data and satellite photographs. She is well known as one of the people who presents our weather forecast on television.

'Enjoy each day as it comes, rain or shine. Look around you and do all you can to keep our world beautiful.

SONIA O'SULLIVAN

Sonia is one of the top athletes in the world today. She has run and won in many countries. Her natural talent and many hours of training tell us clearly that our gifts will only blossom with self belief and hard work.

'The old scholars were quite right when they said, "mens sana in corpore sano – a healthy mind in a healthy body". Keep your minds and bodies healthy and happy.'